painted
woodcraft

painted
woodcraft

STEWART AND SALLY WALTON

photography by David Montgomery

Sterling Publishing Co., Inc.
New York

Designer **Mark Latter**

Editor **Zia Mattocks**

Project Editor **Catherine Ward**

Production Manager **Kate Mackillop**

Illustrator **Michael Hill**

Photographer **David Montgomery**

Library of Congress Cataloging-in-Publication Data Available

1 2 3 4 5 6 7 8 9 10

Published in 1997 by Sterling Publishing Company, Inc
38 Park Avenue South, New York, NY 10016

Originally published in Great Britain in 1997 by Ryland Peters & Small
Cavendish House, 51–55 Mortimer Street, London W1N 7TD

Text © Stewart and Sally Walton 1997
Design and photographs © Ryland Peters & Small 1997

Distributed in Canada by Sterling Publishing
c/o Canadian Manda Group, One Atlantic Avenue, Suite 105, Toronto, Ontario, Canada M6K 3E7

Produced by Mandarin Offset
Printed in Hong Kong

ISBN 0-8069-9582-3

Contents

Introduction

People have been using tools to cut and shape wood since the earliest civilization, and our museums trace the everyday lives of our ancestors through the artifacts that they left behind. Wood has been painted and inlaid with other materials to make it more decorative, or carved with elaborate patterns for ceremonial uses. Looking back, it seems that painting and crafting wood is a natural activity for us humans, and is something for all of us to enjoy at our own particular level of skill.

If you are an experienced woodworker looking for inspiration, or an inspired decorative painter in search of a new surface, or somebody who has never attempted to paint or make anything from wood but would like to make a start—then this is the ideal book for you.

The first chapter contains sumptuous step-by-step photographs which demonstrate the paint styles and effects used in the projects and how to achieve them. The projects themselves are illustrated through all the key stages of assembly and decoration. Also included is a comprehensive guide to all the basic tools, equipment and techniques you will need.

Some of the projects have a painting bias and only need to be cut out of wood, like the clock face and the door numbers. Others, like the spice cupboard, provide more of a challenge to the woodworker; but all the projects have been designed to be made by people with various skill levels. So, even if you have never used a miter box or a crackle glazing varnish before, we hope you will take the plunge. The unfamiliar task provides the biggest challenge and the greatest sense of achievement when successfully completed—so why not try something new? The pleasure of making something should not be underestimated. It is absorbing, uplifting and satisfying to work with your hands, and also therapeutically calming to concentrate on just one thing at a time. The measuring, sawing, assembling or sanding are each separate tasks and performing them can be as rewarding as the end result.

Painted Finishes

The projects in this book should suit people with a wide range of skills, both those with years of experience and those who are just starting out.

There has been a deliberate mystique attached to the whole area of painted finishes for far too long. While it is true that some fine finishes need patience, skill, and a lot of practice, there are others that are very easy, fun to do, and require only basic household decorating materials.

Most of us have a selection of brushes, sandpapers, and drawing equipment, and any hardware or paint store will carry a good selection of paint. You may need to visit an art shop for some of the artists' colors, but they are easy to find and not too expensive.

Gold leafing and crackle glazing can both be done using special products sold in kit form. Their advantage is that they give you everything you need in one small pack, just enough for one or two projects. We have also shown how to do distressing and liming without spending anything but time.

All the finishes covered in the following pages can be done by beginners and experts alike. Those of you who already have experience will know that each project you undertake is a personal adventure and all creativity is a worthwhile pursuit. Nobody is going to grade your work, so do it for your own satisfaction—and enjoy it.

If you are not set up for carpentry—don't be discouraged. It is possible to buy many items similar to those made in this book and just give them the paint treatment. It is particularly satisfying to find an old wooden object in a secondhand store, and then restore and paint it.

Combing

Combed patterns are full of vigor and spontaneity. The effect relies on the glaze being wet and workable, so use it on small items or sections, such as panels of a larger piece. Although you can buy rubber graining combs, it is very simple to cut them out of cardboard yourself. If you are right-handed, comb the paint from left to right, and vice versa if you are left-handed.

MATERIALS AND EQUIPMENT

cutting mat

thick cardboard, such as mat
  board, 4 x 5 inches, for each
  comb

craft knife

paint for base coat, such as matte
  latex paint in a paler color than
  your made-up glaze

oil or water-based glaze made up
  as follows:

  I part paint to I part varnish
  (use artists' oil paint with
  polyurethane varnish, or artists'
  acrylic paint with water-based
  varnish)

shallow white container, for mixing

2 small household paintbrushes

scrap wood

SUGGESTIONS

Suitable for small items, such as:

Sewing Box (page 22)

Key Cupboard (page 51)

Pencil Box (page 69)

Money Box (page 80)

Picture Frames (page 93)

1 On a cutting mat, make several combs by cutting out small triangles from the pieces of thick cardboard. Use a craft knife to cut the notches along one edge only, varying the size and width of the teeth. Apply a coat of base color onto scrap wood for testing, and then onto your chosen item. Allow to dry.

2 Mix an oil- or water-based glaze—acrylic paint with water-based varnish, or oil paint with polyurethane varnish. Shown here is polyurethane varnish plus equal parts of cadmium red and burnt sienna. Try the glaze on the scrap wood first, adding more color or varnish until the effect is right.

3 Use a paintbrush to apply a coat of glaze on top of the base coat. Starting at one edge, comb across the piece, holding the cardboard at 45° and jiggling it up and down to make a wavy pattern. Wipe excess glaze off the cardboard before combing the next row close to the first. Repeat over the entire piece.

4 This simple basketweave effect is applied in the same way, this time combing with straight vertical and horizontal lines. Work in one direction first, then turn the piece and comb across the first pattern at right angles. Use the same comb for even-sized checks, or one with wider teeth for a tartan effect.

Spattering

This paint finish is created by spattering different colors onto an even base color to resemble polished stone. Terra-cottas, grays, and greens produce the most realistic effects. Be warned, however—it can be a messy business, so protect your work surface with newspaper and a cardboard spray-booth, and be prepared to mess up your hands.

1 Construct a spray-booth from a large cardboard box or newspaper. Apply a base coat of terra-cotta latex paint to the whole surface of your piece. Add a second coat to ensure a smooth, opaque covering. Darken the terra-cotta paint by adding an equal part of Venetian red acrylic paint and mixing it well.

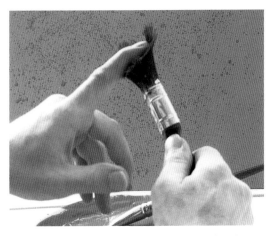

2 Dip a small, clean, dry household paintbrush into the darkened terra-cotta paint mixed in step 1. Hold the brush about 10 to 12 inches away from the surface. Run your finger over the end of the brush, towards yourself, so that the paint flicks onto the surface. Apply an even coat of flicks.

3 To make the paint a lighter pink, add an equal part of white acrylic paint or latex paint to the remaining darkened terra-cotta. Repeat the flicking process with this lighter color until the piece is evenly covered. If you wish, add another color, such as a black or blue, for a more dramatic finish.

4 Seal the paint surface with a coat of shellac to add a golden sheen and provide a thin protective coating. To achieve an even finer finish, smooth with fine sandpaper and seal with a further coat of shellac. For a stronger protective finish, seal with one or more coats of water-based varnish.

MATERIALS AND EQUIPMENT

cardboard box, for spray-booth
terra-cotta latex paint
Venetian red artists' acrylic paint
white artists' acrylic paint or latex paint
black or blue artists' acrylic paint or latex paint (optional)
shellac
water-based varnish (optional)
shallow white container, for mixing
4–5 small household paintbrushes
fine sandpaper

SUGGESTIONS

Do not be tempted to use this finish on a large surface such as a wall—the effect can be optically dazzling. It is better suited to smaller surfaces and can be adapted for many of the items in this book, including:

Letter Rack (page 26)
Money Box (page 80)
Picture Frames (page 93)
Lamp Base (page 112)

Stenciling

Stencils can be as simple or complex as your cutting skills allow, but remember the limitations when choosing your design as all the elements need to be "tied" into the background. Waxed cardboard is cheap and easy to cut, but clear plastic sheeting allows you to position and link your design more accurately. Stenciling has one golden rule—never use too much paint.

MATERIALS AND EQUIPMENT

tracing paper

pencil

spray adhesive

waxed cardboard or sheet of
  clear plastic

cutting mat

craft knife

artists' oil or acrylic paints

polyurethane or water-based
  varnish

stencil brush

absorbent paper

SUGGESTIONS

Stenciling has multiple applications and can even be used on walls and whole rooms. It is suitable for many of the projects in this book, including:

Candle Box (page 36)

Key Cupboard (page 51)

Pull-along Duck (page 62)

Picture Frames (page 93)

Window Box (page 100)

1 Carefully trace your chosen design. Remember that, if necessary, you can photocopy the design to increase its size as required. Spray the back of the sheet of tracing paper with a thin coat of adhesive and stick it onto the waxed cardboard or sheet of plastic, making sure it is square to the edges.

2 Place the cardboard on a cutting mat and cut out the stencil using a sharp craft knife to press through the tracing and into the cardboard or plastic. Follow the design carefully and move the stencil around as you work, so that you are always cutting at the angle that gives you most control over the blade.

3 Spray the back of the stencil with adhesive and position it on your surface. Dip the brush into the first color and rub it on absorbent paper until it is almost dry. Dab the color on with a "pouncing" motion, working from the edges into the middle. Clean the brush and repeat for subsequent colors.

4 Without removing the stencil, gently lift one corner to check that you have used enough color. If not, smooth the stencil into position again and add more color. Do this carefully, so the outlines won't smudge. Allow to dry, then peel off the stencil and apply one or more coats of varnish to seal the paint.

Liming

Although this is not the true liming technique, it does give a similar effect. The surface is scuffed with a wire brush, then covered with a coat of thinned white latex paint. This is sanded off, leaving the grained pattern outlined in chalky white. It is a very easy and accessible way to cheat at liming.

MATERIALS AND EQUIPMENT

small wire brush
2 soft cloths
white latex paint
water-based matte varnish
water
shallow white container, for mixing
small household paintbrush
medium and fine sandpaper
steel wool (optional)

SUGGESTIONS

This technique gives a very attractive aged or country look and is suitable for quite large pieces of furniture, as well as smaller items, such as:

Sewing Box (page 22)

Key Cupboard (page 51)

Picture Frames (page 93)

1 With a small wire brush, brush over the surface of your piece, working in the direction of the grain, raking out and creating channels to catch the paint. This is the most important step—the more channels you create by gouging with the wire brush, the more interesting the final effect will be. Wipe clean.

2 Pour white latex paint into a small container, then add enough water to thin down the mixture to the consistency of thin cream. Stir well. Using a small household paintbrush, apply the paint following the direction of the grain and making sure it fills all the gouged-out crevices. Allow to dry.

3 Using medium sandpaper, sand off the surface paint. Sand again, this time with fine sandpaper, until the only remaining white paint is in the grain. If necessary, rub gently with steel wool to produce a fine, smooth surface. The remaining paint will produce the final limed effect.

4 To add a protective finish, dip a clean soft cloth into matte varnish and apply a thin coat over the entire surface, without allowing it to get into the grain and spoil the chalky effect. Allow to dry. If necessary, sand again and apply a second coat of varnish to produce an even better result.

Lining on Board

Successful lining depends on the right tools and a relaxed, confident and steady hand. Use turpentine and polyurethane varnish to thin oil paints and use water to thin acrylics. A lining brush has long bristles to hold lots of paint, which flows easily down to the tip as you paint the line. Experiment with the lining brush until you get the consistency right.

MATERIALS AND EQUIPMENT

pencil

strip of wood, for straightedge

handsaw

masking tape

2 erasers (optional)

artists' acrylic or oil paint

water (to thin acrylic paint)

turpentine (to thin oil paint)

polyurethane varnish (to thin oil paint)

shallow white container, for mixing

lining brush

scrap wood

SUGGESTIONS

Lining has many applications and can be adapted for large pieces of furniture, as well as several of the projects that are featured in this book, including:

Money Box (page 80)

Window Box (page 100)

Model Boat (page 116)

1 Using a pencil, draw guidelines along the long edge of the wood. Maintain a straight line by keeping your middle finger rigid and sliding it against the side of the wood as you draw the line. This is very good practice for freehand lining with a brush, as shown in step 4.

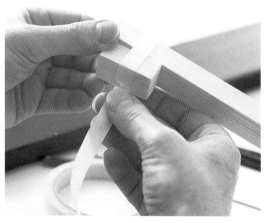

2 Make a raised straightedge out of a strip of wood. Saw two 2-inch pieces from the wood and attach one to each end with masking tape. They will act as "feet" and lift the straightedge clear of the painting surface. Alternatively, you could use erasers, which give a good grip.

3 Thin the paint with water for acrylic paints, or with two parts turpentine to one part varnish for oils. Mix well, then experiment on scrap wood with the lining brush until the paint flows freely without losing too much opacity; practicing this will teach you to move your hand freely and confidently.

4 Place the raised straightedge on the wood ½ inch from your guideline and hold it firmly with your spare hand. Dip the brush into the paint and, resting the handle of the brush against the straightedge, paint a straight line with one single stroke—don't hesitate or the brush will wobble.

Distressing

There are some very effective, though time-consuming ways to distress furniture, like imitating woodworm holes or recreating normal wear and tear. This is a relatively simple way to age a piece and takes very little time. The example shown here is a paneled door, but this process could just as effectively be applied to a wooden toy or a piece of furniture.

MATERIALS AND EQUIPMENT

medium and fine sandpaper
2 soft cloths
latex paint
artists' acrylic paint
water
shallow white container, for mixing
2 small household paintbrushes
antiquing wax

SUGGESTIONS

This is a simple method of achieving a distressed effect for large pieces of furniture or for small objects, such as:

Key Cupboard (page 51)

Pull-along Duck (page 62)

Dolls' House (page 84)

1 Start with bare wood and sand thoroughly, first with medium sandpaper, then with fine. Wipe away the dust with a soft cloth. Use a small household paintbrush to apply a base coat of latex paint directly onto the sanded wood. Allow to dry thoroughly before proceeding to the next step.

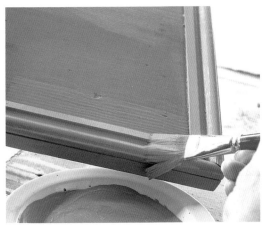

2 Make up the second color by mixing three parts acrylic paint to one part latex paint in a shallow white container. Then add one part water to produce a thinner consistency. Using a clean paintbrush, apply an even coat over the base coat and allow to dry.

3 Using fine sandpaper, rub back the top coat so the base coat color shows through in places. Exaggerate the effect in areas where most natural wear would occur by taking off the base coat as well, revealing some of the bare wood underneath. Aim for a graduated effect with no hard edges.

4 Finish with a coat of antiquing wax, applied with a soft cloth. Antiquing wax is tinted beeswax, which is rubbed on and then buffed off to leave a subtle sheen, a slightly darker color, and a heavenly aroma. It also protects any areas of bare wood that are exposed during the distressing process.

Crackle Glazing

This effect is amazingly easy to achieve, especially now you can buy the materials in kit form. These contain two types of varnish—a base coat and a top coat—which dry at different rates, so the top one shrinks and crackles while the base is left intact. Dark oil paint is then rubbed into the cracks to highlight them. Shown here is fine, dark crackling on a pale background.

MATERIALS AND EQUIPMENT

paint for base coat, such as cream
  latex paint
crackle glazing kit, consisting of:
  base coat varnish
  crackling varnish
artists' oil paint, such as burnt
  umber
paint thinner (optional)
polyurethane varnish
2 soft cloths
3 paintbrushes, as appropriate

SUGGESTIONS

This attractive finish can be used
on larger items of furniture that
are comprised of smaller sections,
such as small tables, chests of
drawers and chairs, or on some of
the smaller items in this book,
including:

Candle Box (page 36)

Plate Rack (page 43)

Key Cupboard (page 51)

Picture Frames (page 93)

1 First paint your piece with a base coat, choosing a color that will contrast well with the oil paint used to fill in the cracks in the crackling varnish (see step 3). Here, cream latex paint has been used to contrast with burnt umber artists' oil paint. When the paint is dry, apply a coat of the clear base varnish.

2 (Not shown) Allow the base coat varnish to dry completely. Then, following the manufacturer's instructions, apply a coat of the crackling varnish over the top. As it dries, angle the piece towards the light and you should be able to see the top coat of varnish starting to crackle.

3 (Above) Using a soft cloth, apply a thin coat of oil paint over the surface, rubbing it well into the cracks and corners. The color used here is burnt umber, which gives the wood a beautiful aged appearance.

4 Using a clean cloth, rub all the paint off the surface so it just remains in the cracks. If you can't shift the paint, dampen the cloth with paint thinner and try again. Do not overdo this because it will run into the cracks and spoil the effect.

5 Finally, to seal and protect the crackled surface, apply a coat of clear polyurethane varnish.

Varnishing

A final coat of varnish improves most painted surfaces—colors are enhanced and details brought into focus. Choose either a solvent-based polyurethane varnish, which is clear and tough, or a water-based acrylic one, which is milky when liquid but clear when dry. Always use good-quality, clean, broad brushes for varnishing. A 1-inch artist's brush is ideal.

1 Clear Varnish Load one-third of the brush with varnish, removing the excess against the inside of the can—don't drag it across the rim as that promotes bubbles. Gently apply each coat in the direction of the grain, dabbing a small blob in the center and brushing half of it away from you and the rest towards you.

2 Tinted Varnish Use a white container for mixing so you can see the color clearly. Pour the varnish onto the container first, then gradually add the color with a brush until you achieve the required intensity. Mix water-based varnish with acrylic paints and polyurethane varnish with oils. Apply as for clear varnish.

3 Changing Colors Tinted varnishes are useful if you want to change the color of your painted wood, for example, you could coat a yellow object with blue varnish to produce green. This technique can also be used to brighten or soften the underlying color. To mix tinted varnishes, see above right.

4 Antiquing Varnish Tinted brown or yellow, antiquing varnish can be used to darken or dull the wood color, giving it an aged look. Apply as for clear varnish, making sure it goes into all the crevices and corners. To create a distressed, naturally worn look, wipe off the varnish with a cloth before it is fully dry.

MATERIALS AND EQUIPMENT

varnish, as required
colored paint, for tinted varnish
antiquing varnish, available in
  shades describing types of
  wood, such as dark oak
shallow white container, for mixing
paintbrushes, as appropriate
cloth

SUGGESTIONS

Most painted pieces can be improved by one or more coats of varnish, including:

Decorations (page 96)

Money Box (page 80)

Model Boat (page 116)

MATERIALS AND EQUIPMENT

red oxide primer

gold size (an adhesive for metallic
    powders and leaf)

1–2 books gold leaf or Dutch
    metal (25 sheets each)

shellac

3 small household paintbrushes

fine steel wool

SUGGESTIONS

This easy-to-achieve effect is
particularly suited to small,
decorative items including:

Money Box (page 80)

Picture Frames (page 93)

Gold Leafing

*Gilding has never been easier. Hobby kits, sold in art and craft shops, can be used
to apply a glimmering gold finish to small flat objects such as this simple picture frame.
Traditional water gilding is a highly skilled craft, but gold size and metal leaf can be used
even by inexperienced painters to achieve quite professional-looking results.*

1 Following the wood grain, apply red oxide primer
with a small paintbrush. Allow to dry for about an
hour. Apply gold size with a clean brush and let this
become tacky enough to bind the sheets of gold leaf
or Dutch metal, one at a time, on top. Overlap each
sheet slightly until the frame is completely covered.

2 Use a clean, dry paintbrush to remove the excess
gold leaf. The resulting effect is deliberately patchy,
with areas of red oxide showing through the gold.
If there are any awkward gaps remaining, carefully
apply more gold leaf on top to cover them, as
described in step 1.

3 The next process is to distress the surface of the
gold leaf to lend the object an authentic antique
look. Start by rubbing the gold area firmly with a
piece of fine steel wool—this will burnish the surface
to give it an aged appearance, but it will not remove
any of the gold leaf.

4 To finish off the effect, use a small household
paintbrush to apply a coat of shellac on top of the
burnished gold leaf. Shellac has a warm, yellowish
golden tint, so it will enhance the gilded surface
of your chosen piece, as well as providing it with
a protective seal.

Wood Graining

In the hands of a skilled painter, wood graining can look amazingly authentic. However, this simple approach is impressionistic, rather than being realistic. It needs no specialist tools—just a bold hand and a dry household paintbrush. This particular pattern should result in a mottled, close-grained wood effect.

1 Begin by sanding the wood with fine sandpaper to provide a surface for keying the paint. Wipe the wood clean with a soft cloth, then apply the base coat. Mix up a glaze in the proportions listed (right). Linseed oil—which will keep the paint workable—should be added slowly and last of all.

2 Take a small amount of glaze onto a dry brush and paint it onto your wood, always working in the direction of the grain. Starting at the edge nearest to you, hold the brush vertically and "walk" it away from you, pushing the brush down slightly to work the glaze into the grain.

3 Continue to cover the surface of the wood with glaze. Then, while it is still wet, press a clean, dry paintbrush flat onto the painted surface. Drag the brush towards you, moving it from side to side in an irregular motion to imitate wood grain. For example, parallel lines can be used to simulate pine.

4 To create a pattern that resembles the knots in wood, use the same method as before, but this time work heavier patches of glaze into the surface, building it up in layers to create areas with a more solid appearance. Then, with the tip of a dry brush, use a swirling motion to make the grained pattern.

MATERIALS AND EQUIPMENT

fine sandpaper

soft cloth

neutral-colored paint, for base coat

wood graining glaze mixture:

    1 part cadmium red artists' oil paint

    1 part burnt umber artists' oil paint

    1 part polyurethane varnish

    1–2 drops linseed oil (optional)

shallow white container, for mixing

3 or 4 small household paintbrushes

SUGGESTIONS

This impressionistic finish is suitable for items such as:

Spice Chest (page 46)

Key Cupboard (page 51)

Dolls' House (page 84)

Window Box (page 100)

Home Crafts

SEWING BOX

This chunky little box with a drawer and two compartments makes a perfect sewing box. The wood grain shows through the sanded base coat and adds another level of interest to the painted pattern.

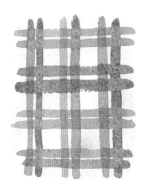

YOU WILL NEED

MATERIALS FOR BOX

½-inch reclaimed wood, such as
    floorboards, or softwood, cut as
    follows:
two 6½ x 12 inches, for front and
    back
two 6½ x 5 inches, for sides
two approximately 11 x 5 inches,
    for base of box and base of top
    compartment (cut to fit)
one 13 x 7 inches, for lid top
¼-inch softwood, cut as follows:
two 2½ x 5 inches, for base supports
one 2½ x 5 inches, for divider
one 10⅞ x 4⅞ inches, for inside lid
approximately ¼-x-½-inch half-astragal
    molding, 45-inch length, to surround
    base

MATERIALS FOR DRAWER

¼-inch softwood, cut as follows:
two 2 x 7¾ inches, for back and
    inner front
two 2 x 5½ inches, for sides
one 2½ x 8¾ inches, for false front
one approximately 7¾ x 5 inches,
    for base (cut to fit)
small knob (with screw)

TOOLS AND EQUIPMENT

pencil and ruler
clamps
saber saw and tenon saw
wood glue
1-inch nails, finishing nails and hammer
medium and fine sandpaper
plane
bradawl and screwdriver
miter box

1 Start by marking the position for the drawer on the front piece of the box, using a pencil and ruler. The opening measures 2 x 8¼ inches and should be placed centrally ¾ inch above the base. Using clamps, secure the wood to a table-top or workbench and cut out the slot with a saber saw.

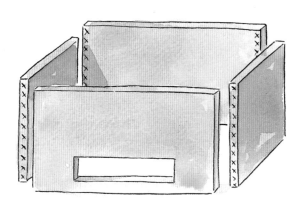

2 Assemble the box with wood glue, butting the sides up to the back, and reinforce with 1-inch nails from the back. Then do the same for the front.

3 Cut the base of the box to fit inside the assembled sides. Apply wood glue to the side edges of the base and insert it inside the box, flush with the bottom, and secure it with nails from the outside.

4 Apply wood glue to each edge and to one side of the base supports, then insert them inside the box against the side pieces so that they sit on the base. Clamp until the glue has bonded. Cut the base of the top compartment to fit inside the box. Apply glue along the bottom edge of the top compartment where it will meet the base supports, then insert it into the box so that it sits on the supports.

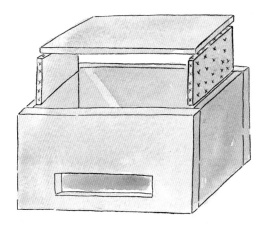

5 To insert the divider in the correct position, first measure and mark the center of the front and back pieces. Apply wood glue to the bottom and side edges of the divider and glue it into the box at the center marks so that it sits on the base of the top compartment, dividing it into two equal sections. The divider will not reach right up to the top edge of the box, allowing room for the inner lid.

6 Take the two pieces of wood that form the lid. Center the smaller one on the larger one and glue them together. Use clamps to hold the two layers in place while the glue sets.

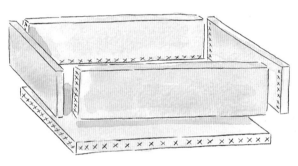

7 Smooth any rough edges on the top lid with medium and fine sandpaper, rounding the edges slightly. Then position the lid over the box to check that it can be lifted on and off with ease. If necessary, smooth the edges of the inner lid with sandpaper.

8 Assemble the drawer with glue, butting the front and back up to the sides, and secure with nails. Place the drawer frame on the wood for the base and mark around the inside edges to give the exact dimensions of the base, then cut it out. Apply wood glue to the edges of the base and position it in the drawer. Reinforce with nails from the outside.

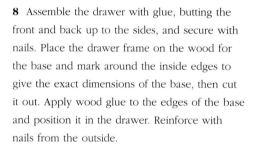

9 Use a plane and sandpaper to bevel the edges of the false front. Glue it centrally over the front of the drawer with a ¼-inch overlap all around. Make a pilot hole for the knob with a bradawl and screw it in place. Check the fit of the drawer and sand the edges if necessary until it opens and closes smoothly.

10 Using a miter box and tenon saw, cut the half-astragal molding into four sections to fit around the base of the box, mitering the corners at 45°. Apply wood glue, then fit the sections of molding together around the sides of the box, making sure that they are flush with the bottom edges to provide a steady base, then nail them in place.

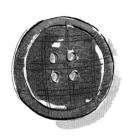

PAINT PALETTE AND EQUIPMENT

white acrylic primer
artists' acrylic paints in the
    following colors:
    Indian red
    ultramarine
water-based matte varnish
shallow white container, for mixing
No. 6 lining brush
triangle
strip of cardboard, ⅜ inch wide
varnishing brush

PAINT SWATCH

Blue

    1 part Indian red
    5 parts ultramarine
    6 parts water-based varnish

STEPS TO PAINT

1 Paint the whole box and drawer (inside and out) with white acrylic primer. Let dry.

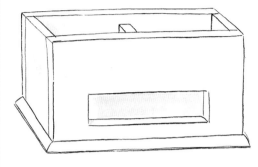

2 Using medium sandpaper, rub back the surface until the white shows only where it remains caught in the grain of the wood.

3 Mix the blue paint to match the swatch. If the mixture is too thick, add water so that the paint flows easily off the brush, giving a translucent effect.

4 The pattern is made up of pairs of horizontal and vertical blue stripes, made with a single stroke, the same thickness as the No. 6 lining brush.

Paint two vertical stripes about ⅛ inch apart. If necessary, use a triangle to help keep your lines vertical. Using your cardboard marker as a guide, paint a second pair ⅜ inch from the first. Repeat this process around the four sides of the box.

5 Leave the vertical lines to dry, then paint the horizontal lines. It is easier to keep your lines straight if you paint from top to bottom, so stand the box on its side, propping up the top end to compensate for the height of the molding, then work the same pattern across the width of the box.

6 As a finishing touch, paint the small knob with the same blue paint. If necessary, roughen up the wood first with sandpaper to create an absorbent surface ready for painting. When the paint is dry, coat the box with water-based matte varnish.

LETTER RACK

A letter rack like this will help you to keep track of your correspondence, with compartments for both incoming and outgoing letters. Make it out of fiberboard, with beading to decorate the base.

YOU WILL NEED

MATERIALS

sufficient ¼-inch fiberboard to cut
the following pieces:

one 2⅞ x 9 inches, for front

one 6¹⁄₁₆ x 9 inches, for back

one 4⅜ x 8½ inches, for central
divider

two 4½ x 2¾ inches, for sides

one approximately 9 x 3¼ inches,
for base (cut to fit)

approximately ½-inch triangular
beading or picture-frame molding,
25-inch length, to surround three
sides of base

TOOLS AND EQUIPMENT

tracing paper

pencil

clamps

saber saw

medium and fine sandpaper

wood glue

finishing nails

hammer

tenon saw

miter box

1 Trace the templates on page 29 and transfer the shapes onto the fiberboard. Clamp the wood to a workbench or tabletop, then cut out the shapes with a saber saw. Sand the rough edges.

2 To assemble the rack, apply wood glue and butt the sides up to the back and front pieces. Clamp these joints until the glue has bonded, then reinforce with finishing nails tapped through from the front and back into the sides.

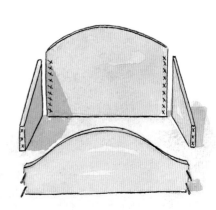

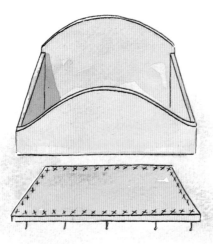

3 To obtain the exact measurement of the base, place the assembled rack on the fiberboard and mark the dimensions around the outside of the rack. Cut out the base, apply glue to the lower edges of the rack and clamp it in position. Nail through from underneath to reinforce.

4 Mark the position of the central divider. Apply wood glue to the lower and side edges and slip it into position (see below).

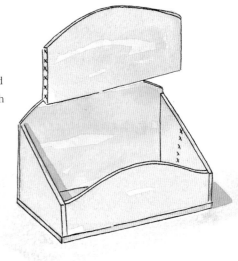

5 Using a tenon saw, cut the beading or molding to fit around the front and sides of the base, mitering the corners at 45° with a miter box so that the beading fits snugly around the rack.

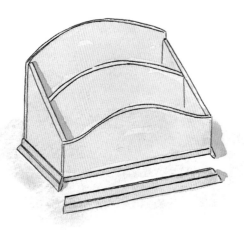

6 Glue the beading in position, placing the rack on a flat surface so that the base is level. Then clamp in position until the glue has bonded.

PAINT PALETTE AND EQUIPMENT

white acrylic primer

artists' acrylic paints in the following
  colors:
  chocolate brown
  Venetian red
  ultramarine
  black
  white
  gray
water-based satin varnish
shallow white container, for mixing
broad long-handled paintbrush
cardboard box, for spray-booth
stiff-bristled paintbrush
varnishing brush

PAINT SWATCHES

Chocolate brown

Venetian red

Blue-black (optional)
  3 parts ultramarine
  1 part black

Pink
  3 parts Venetian red
  1 part white

Gray
  3 parts gray
  1 part ultramarine

STEPS TO PAINT

1 Paint the whole rack with white acrylic primer, using a broad long-handled paintbrush to get down into the divisions. Let dry.

2 Again using a long-handled brush, apply the chocolate brown base coat and let dry.

3 Make a simple spray-booth out of a large cardboard box.

4 Practice your spattering technique on scrap paper: load the stiff-bristled paintbrush with paint, then run your finger across the top to flick dots of paint onto the surface. Some dots will be bigger than others, but try not to make them too big or the paint will run and spoil the effect.

Flick first with Venetian red, then with a blue-black, if you decide to use it, then with pink, and finally with gray. Let dry.

5 When you are satisfied with the overall effect, apply two coats of water-based satin varnish according to the manufacturer's instructions.

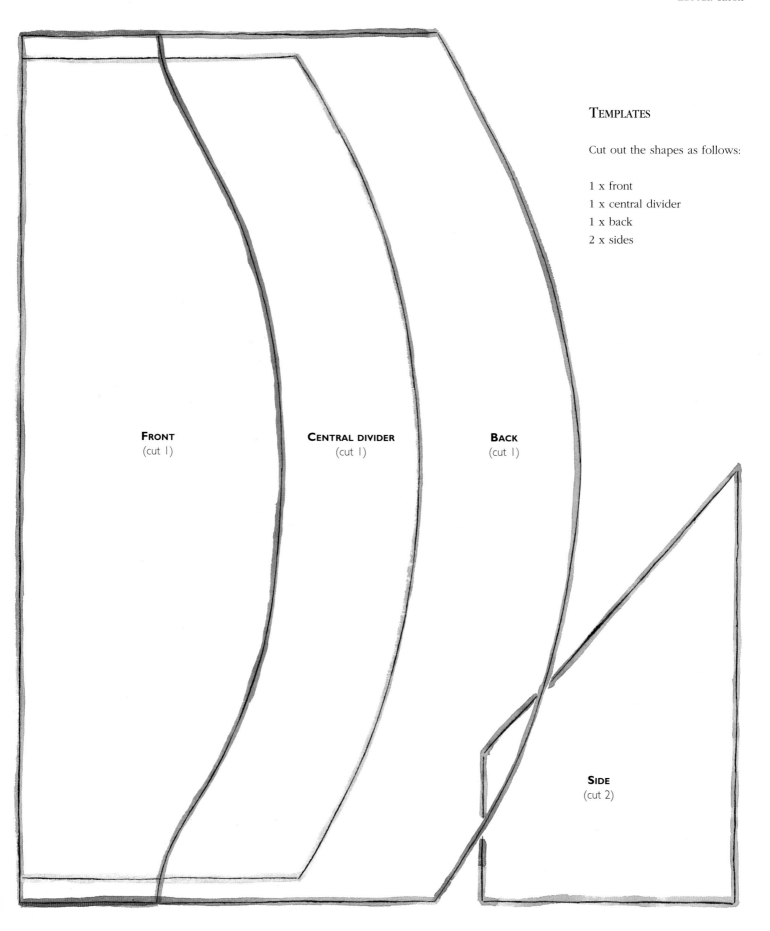

FRONT
(cut 1)

CENTRAL DIVIDER
(cut 1)

BACK
(cut 1)

TEMPLATES

Cut out the shapes as follows:

1 x front
1 x central divider
1 x back
2 x sides

SIDE
(cut 2)

GARDENING BASKET

The design on this gardening basket was inspired by early Pennsylvania Dutch toleware, which was practical as well as decorative. The pattern is a celebration of freehand brushstrokes with the outlines and highlights added later to pull the whole design together.

YOU WILL NEED

MATERIALS

sufficient ½-inch softwood to cut the
  following pieces:
  two 3¾ x 15⅝ inches, for sides
  two 3¾ x 10¼ inches, for ends
  one 4½ x 14⅝ inches, for central
    divider
¼-x-¼-inch softwood, two 10¼-inch
  lengths and two 14⅛-inch lengths,
    for ledge
¼-inch plywood, 14⅝ x 10¼ inches,
  for base

TOOLS AND EQUIPMENT

wood glue
finishing nails
hammer
tracing paper
pencil
clamps
saber saw
drill
ruler
medium and fine sandpaper

1 Using wood glue, join the four side pieces together,
butting the shortest ends up to the longest sides.

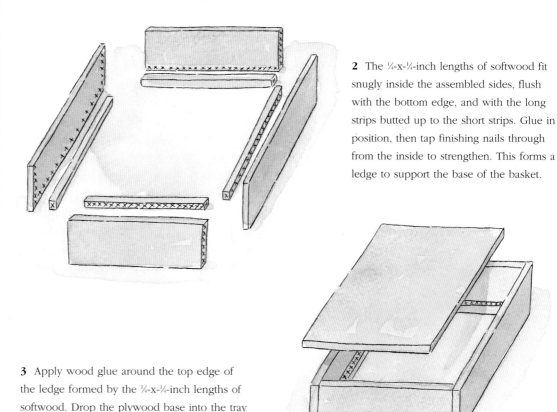

2 The ¼-x-¼-inch lengths of softwood fit
snugly inside the assembled sides, flush
with the bottom edge, and with the long
strips butted up to the short strips. Glue in
position, then tap finishing nails through
from the inside to strengthen. This forms a
ledge to support the base of the basket.

3 Apply wood glue around the top edge of
the ledge formed by the ¼-x-¼-inch lengths of
softwood. Drop the plywood base into the tray
so that it rests on the ledge. Let dry.

4 Trace the template for the central divider from pages 32–3 and transfer the
shape onto the remaining piece of softwood. Clamp the wood onto a
tabletop or workbench and cut out the curved top edge and the shape for
the handle with a saber saw, drilling a hole first to take the blade of the saw.

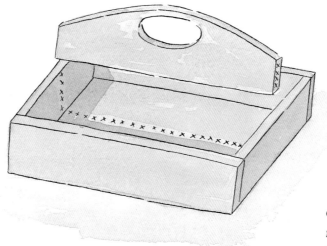

5 Mark the position of the
central divider on the short ends
of the basket. Apply glue and
slide the divider into position.
For added strength tap finishing
nails through from the outside
to hold it firmly in place.

6 Before you paint and varnish the
gardening basket, smooth the cut edges
with medium and fine sandpaper.

PAINT PALETTE AND EQUIPMENT

white acrylic primer

artists' acrylic paints in the following colors:

  white

  cobalt blue

  raw umber

  sap green

  ultramarine

  cadmium yellow light

  vermilion

  cadmium red

water-based satin varnish

turpentine

shallow white container, for mixing

broad household paintbrush

No. 8 artists' brush

No. 5 lining brush

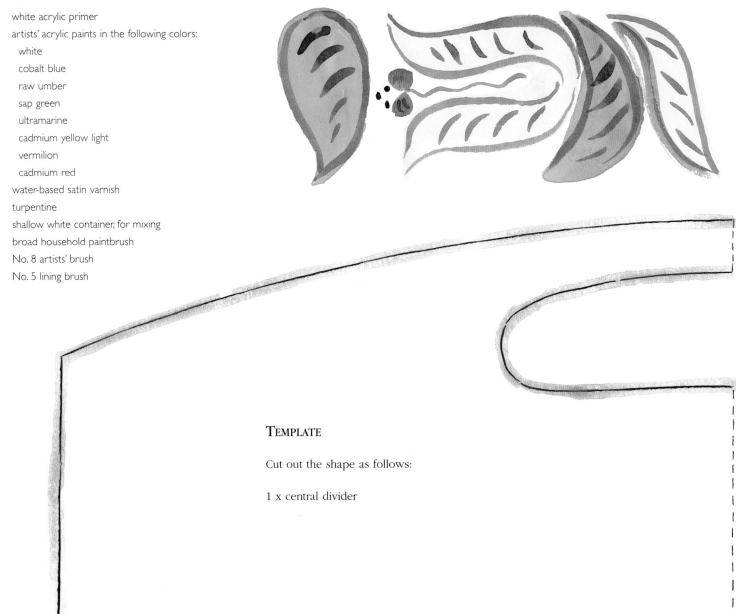

TEMPLATE

Cut out the shape as follows:

1 x central divider

STEPS TO PAINT

1 Prime the basket inside and out with white acrylic primer and allow to dry.

2 Using a broad household paintbrush, apply a base coat of gray to the entire basket and allow it to dry.

3 Trace the leaf and flower shapes on the opposite page and transfer them onto the sides of the basket with a pencil.

4 Using a No. 8 artists' brush, paint the leaves green. Allow to dry.

5 Paint the remaining shapes yellow and leave to dry.

6 Now paint over some of the yellow areas with red paint and leave to dry.

7 Using a No. 5 lining brush, outline all the painted shapes with blue-black and draw in the details, such as the leaf veins.

8 When you are happy with the external decoration, paint the inside of the box with the same blue-black mixture. Do one side at a time, dabbing the wet paint to create a pattern. Allow to dry overnight.

9 Sand all over with fine sandpaper, apply a coat of varnish to seal the paint, and sand again. Apply one final coat of varnish.

PAINT SWATCHES

All the paint mixtures below are thinned with 2 parts varnish to 1 part water.

Gray
2 parts white
1 part cobalt blue
1 part raw umber

Green
3 parts sap green
2 parts white
1 part ultramarine
dash of raw umber

Yellow
2 parts cadmium yellow light
1 part white

Red
1 part vermilion
1 part cadmium red

Blue-black
1 part ultramarine
1 part raw umber

CENTRAL DIVIDER
(cut 1)

33

BOOK BOX

A book box is handy for keeping letters and cards but could equally well be used to store stationery or even jewelry. It looks good displayed on a desk but could also be slotted into a bookshelf where its contents would remain hidden from prying eyes.

YOU WILL NEED

MATERIALS

¼-inch softwood, cut as follows:
   two 10½ x 5 inches, for lid and
      base (front and back covers)
   one 2½ x 10½ inches, for back
      (spine)
½-inch softwood, cut as follows and
   mitered as in step 3:
   two 2½ x 4⅜ inches, for short ends
      (top and bottom edge of pages)
   one 2½ x 9¾ inches, for front
      (front edge of pages)

TOOLS AND EQUIPMENT

pencil
ruler
clamps
saber saw
medium half-round file
medium and fine sandpaper
2 butt hinges (with screws)
craft knife
tenon saw
chisel
mallet
bradawl
screwdriver
wood glue
miter box

PAINT PALETTE AND EQUIPMENT

beige satin-finish latex paint
alizarin crimson artists' oil color
dark oak wood stain
cream latex paint
polyurethane matte varnish
masking tape
1-inch household paintbrush
cloth
varnishing brush

1 Start by marking out he lid on the top section. Draw one pencil line 1 inch in from a long edge and two more 1¼ inches in from each short edge. Using clamps, attach the wood to a tabletop or workbench and cut out this shape with a saber saw. Round off the edges with a file and sandpaper so that the lid will open and close smoothly.

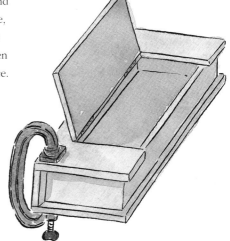

2 Position the hinges as shown and draw around them with a craft knife. Using a chisel and mallet, make hinge mortises by hollowing out a recess to their depth so that they lie flat when in place. Make holes for the screws with a bradawl and fix the hinges in position.

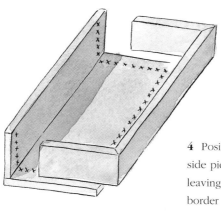

3 To assemble the box, butt the back onto the base and glue in place. Using a miter box and tenon saw, cut both ends of the front piece and one end of the side pieces at 45°. Glue the mitered ends together as shown.

4 Position the front and side pieces on the base, leaving an even ⅜-inch border on all sides, then glue and clamp in place.

5 Apply glue to the top edge of the back and side pieces and lower the top section onto it, making sure it lines up with the base. Secure with clamps until the glue has bonded. To finish, use the file and sandpaper to round off the edges of the assembled box.

STEPS TO PAINT

Before you start painting the box, cover the front and sides with masking tape.

1 Using a 1-inch household paintbrush, apply a thick coat of beige satin-finish latex paint to the entire box (inside and out). Use the brush to obtain a grained effect by holding it on its side and dabbing the paint onto the surface. Allow to dry overnight.

2 Paint on a thick layer of alizarin crimson artists' oil color, using a stippling action. Allow to dry for several hours, then skim some of the paint off the surface with a cloth. Let dry overnight.

3 Apply a coat of dark oak wood stain.

4 When dry, remove the masking tape from the pages and apply a coat of cream latex paint. Allow to dry, then paint with dark oak wood stain, using the brush to achieve a streaked effect that simulates the pages of a book.

5 Varnish the outside of the book box with polyurethane matte varnish.

PAINT SWATCH
Alizarin crimson

CANDLE BOX

The design for this box was taken from an 18th-century Pennsylvania Dutch salt box. Nowadays, the scale of the box makes it more suitable for storing candles, since salt is used much more sparingly than in the past.

YOU WILL NEED

MATERIALS FOR BOX

sufficient ½-inch softwood to cut the
following pieces:
two 8 x 5 inches, for sides
one 10 x 13⅝ inches, for back
two approximately 13⅝ x 4½ inches,
for bases (cut to fit)
one 2 x 13⅝ inches, for fixed front
panel
one 13⅝ x 5¼ inches, for lid
¼-inch doweling, two 1¼-inch lengths,
to hinge lid

MATERIALS FOR DRAWER

½-inch softwood, cut as follows:
two 2¼ x 13⅜ inches, for front and
back
two 2¼ x 3½ inches, for sides
one 12⅞ x 3¼ inches, for base
small knob (with screw)

TOOLS AND EQUIPMENT

tracing paper
pencil
clamps
saber saw or coping saw
tenon saw
drill with ¾-inch spade bit and ¼-inch
twist bit
wood glue
finishing nails
hammer
ruler
plane or half-round file
medium and fine sandpaper
craft knife
router or ½-inch chisel and mallet
bradawl
screwdriver

1 Using a photocopier, enlarge the templates on page 39 by 150%. Trace the shapes and transfer them onto the pieces of wood. Clamp the wood to a tabletop or workbench and cut out the two sides and the back, using a saber saw or coping saw for the curves and a tenon saw for the straight ends.

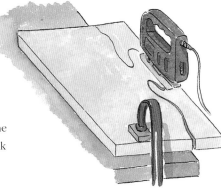

2 Smooth all the rough edges with medium and fine sandpaper. Then drill the decorative hole in the back piece with a ¾-inch spade bit.

3 To assemble the box, first butt the back up to the sides. Glue, then strengthen with finishing nails. Cut the bases to fit inside the box and butt the lower one up to the sides and back, then glue and nail. Draw a pencil line along the back and sides of the box, 2¼ inches from the base. Glue the lower edge of the base of the top compartment along this marked line, parallel with the base of the box. Cut out the fixed front panel and glue it vertically onto this base and reinforce with finishing nails.

4 Use a plane or file to shape the long edges of the lid piece so that it will fit at the correct angle against the back and the front panel. Mark the positions for the dowel hinges on the edges of the lid and on the sides, then use a ¼-inch bit to drill the holes through the sides and to a depth of about ⅜ inch into the edges of the lid. Insert the dowels to hinge the lid and sand the protruding ends level with the sides of the box. Lastly, round the front edge of the lid with sandpaper.

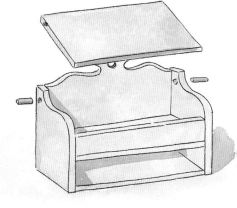

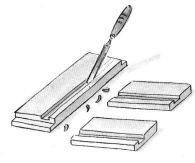

5 For the drawer, either use a router or a chisel and mallet to make a rabbet ½ inch across by ¼ inch deep down both sides of the front and back pieces on the inside. If you use a chisel and mallet, clamp the wood and score a line ½ inch from each side edge, saw to a depth of ¼ inch before chiseling away the waste wood. To make grooves for the base to slot into, either use a router or a chisel and mallet. Make the grooves ½ inch across by ¼ inch deep, ¼ inch from the bottom of the front, back, and side pieces.

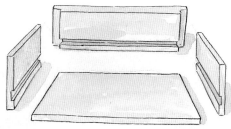

6 To assemble the drawer, glue the sides to the rabbets in the drawer front. Strengthen the joint with finishing nails, tapping them in through the sides so they don't show on the front.

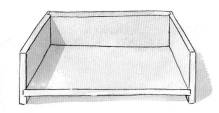

7 Apply glue to the base and slide it into place, then reinforce with finishing nails down each side.

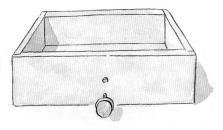

8 Glue the back to the base and sides and nail in place. Make a pilot hole at the front with a bradawl and screw in the small knob.

37

PAINT PALETTE AND EQUIPMENT

white acrylic primer

artists' acrylic paints in the following colors:

   golden ochre

   cadmium red deep

   Venetian red

   sap green

   white

   yellow ochre

   burnt umber

   cadmium yellow deep

water-based matte varnish

shallow white container, for mixing

broad household paintbrush

½-inch and ¼-inch square-tipped

   artists' brushes

soft cloth

spray adhesive

stencil cardboard or sheet of clear

   plastic

stencil brush

No. 4 artists' brush

varnishing brush

PAINT SWATCHES

Golden ochre

Red
   2 parts cadmium red deep
   1 part Venetian red

Sap green

Off-white
   2 parts white
   1 part yellow ochre
   1 part burnt umber

Yellow
   1 part yellow ochre
   1 part cadmium yellow deep

STEPS TO PAINT

1 Prime the whole box with white acrylic primer, using a broad household paintbrush.

2 Paint the entire box, including the drawer front, with a base coat of golden ochre. Leave to dry.

3 Paint the red areas with a ½-inch square-tipped artists' brush and allow to dry.

4 Paint the green edging with a ¼-inch square-tipped brush and leave to dry for a few minutes, before wiping over the surface with a slightly damp soft cloth, so the color becomes transparent and the yellow shows through, especially at the edges.

5 Trace the stencil patterns on the opposite page from the enlarged photocopy. Lightly spray the backs of the tracings with adhesive. Stick them onto the stencil cardboard or sheet of plastic and cut out the shapes with a craft knife.

6 Using the stencil brush, stencil the shapes with off-white paint and allow to dry.

7 Using a No. 4 artists' brush, paint on the yellow dots around the stenciled motifs, then leave to dry overnight before varnishing.

8 Apply a coat of water-based matte varnish.

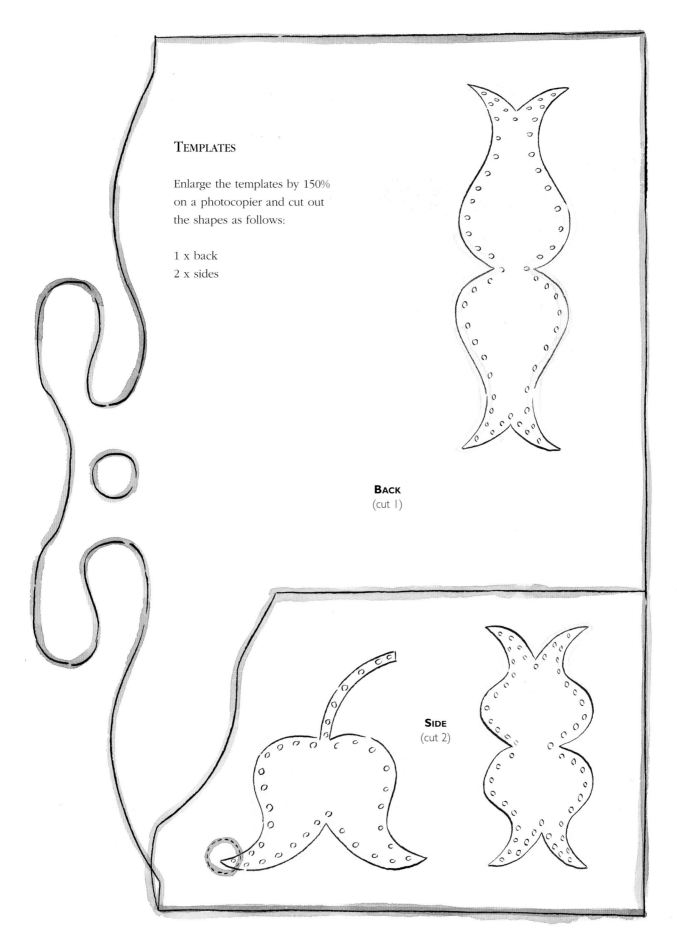

TEMPLATES

Enlarge the templates by 150%
on a photocopier and cut out
the shapes as follows:

1 x back
2 x sides

BACK
(cut 1)

SIDE
(cut 2)

In the Kitchen

PLATE RACK

This is a traditional Swedish-style plate rack, which would have been used to display the family's finest plates. Artists' acrylic paints have been used to create a bold faux marble pattern finished with a coat of wax antiquing polish.

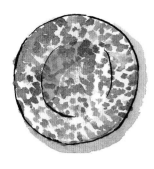

1 On a photocopier, enlarge the template for the two sides on pages 44–5 by 200% and transfer the shape onto each of the two rectangular side pieces, making sure you mark the shelf positions on the inside faces. Clamp each piece of wood in turn to the edge of a sturdy workbench or tabletop and cut out the shapes using a coping saw or saber saw. Sand the sawn curves smooth to remove any jagged edges.

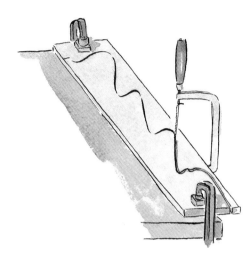

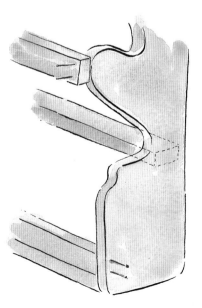

2 The shelves sit between the shaped sides, flush with the straight back edge. Attach them using wood glue and finishing nails, inserted from the outside of the side sections. Start with the wider bottom shelf, positioning it level with the bottom edges of the sides. Next, attach the three remaining shelves, lining them up with the marks made in step 1. Use a try square to check that they are square to the sides.

3 Finally, glue and nail the rails in position. This is done working from the front. Start with the bottom rail, fitting it in between the two sides and flush with the front edge of the bottom shelf to form a step. The other four rails are fitted on the outside edges of the curved sides; position three of them across each of the widest sections of the top three curves and set the final one at the very top of the rack, tucking it behind the highest curve. The position of both shelves and rails can be adjusted to fit any size of plate so that you can have smaller plates on the higher shelves, for example; simply raise or lower them to a suitable height to house your display.

YOU WILL NEED

MATERIALS

sufficient ¾-x-6-inch reclaimed wood, such as floorboards, or softwood to cut the following pieces:
two 32-inch lengths, for sides
one 24-inch length, for bottom shelf

¾-x-2-inch reclaimed wood or softwood, cut as follows:
three 24-inch lengths, for shelves

½-x-1-inch softwood, cut as follows:
four 25½-inch length, for rails
one 24-inch length, for bottom rail

TOOLS AND EQUIPMENT

tracing paper
pencil
clamps
coping saw or saber saw
medium and fine sandpaper
wood glue
finishing nails
hammer
try square
bradawl
4 wall attachments (with screws)
screwdriver

PAINT PALETTE AND EQUIPMENT

white acrylic primer

artists' acrylic paints in the following

  colors:

    ultramarine

    raw umber

    white

    yellow ochre

    vermilion

water

water-based matte varnish

dark oak wax antiquing polish

shallow white container, for mixing

broad artists' brush

No. 2 lining brush

fine-grade steel wool

varnishing brush

soft cloth

PAINT SWATCHES

Blue

  3 parts ultramarine

  1 part raw umber

  1 part white

Dark blue

  1 part ultramarine

  1 part raw umber

Brown-red

  3 parts yellow ochre

  2 parts vermilion

STEPS TO PAINT

1 Paint the entire plate rack with a coat of white acrylic primer and allow to dry.

2 Using a broad artists' brush, paint the whole unit blue, following the first paint swatch.

3 Use your middle finger to steady your pencil and draw in the edge of the border band.

4 Using the No. 2 lining brush and the dark blue mixture, paint squiggly, parallel, diagonal lines all over the plate rack, then repeat this process across the lines you have just made to form a lattice pattern. Thin the paint with water if necessary.

5 Paint the brown-red border and allow to dry overnight.

6 Rub the rack all over with sandpaper and fine-grade steel wool to achieve a smooth surface.

7 Apply one coat of water-based matte varnish in even strokes, using a clean varnishing brush.

8 Finally, apply the tinted wax antiquing polish, buffing with a soft cloth for a professional finish.

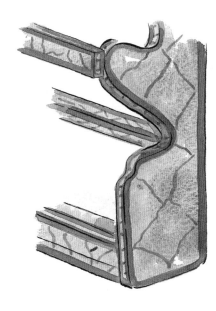

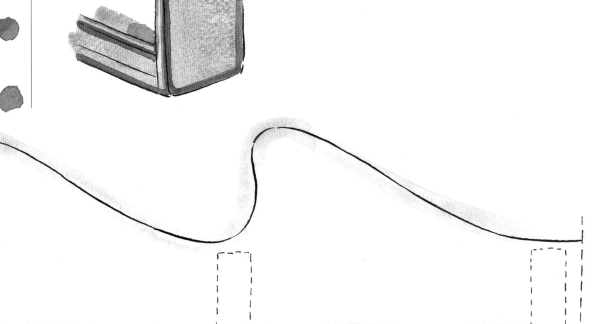

HANGING THE PLATE RACK

1 Using a bradawl, make pilot holes in each corner on the back of the plate rack to take the screws for the wall attachments.

3 Hold the plate rack against the wall and make a mark where the wall screws should go. Fix the screws to the wall, leaving ⅜ inch protruding. Hang the plate rack on the wall and display your plates on the shelves, placing the largest ones on the bottom shelf.

2 Insert the screws into the prepared holes and, using a screwdriver, secure the wall attachments in place on the back of the plate rack.

SIDE
(cut 2)

TEMPLATE

Enlarge the template by 200% on a photocopier and cut out the shape as follows:

2 x sides

SPICE CHEST

This spice chest can be made by anyone with basic tools and good measuring skills. The drawer knobs are cut-down chess pawns. The top pediment reflects the shape of the front pedestal—both are cut from the same piece of wood.

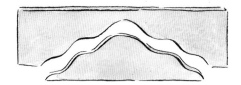

1 Trace the templates from page 49 and transfer them onto the softwood. Clamp the wood to a tabletop, then cut out the shapes using a coping saw for the curved edges and a tenon saw for the straight ends. Sand any rough edges.

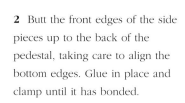

2 Butt the front edges of the side pieces up to the back of the pedestal, taking care to align the bottom edges. Glue in place and clamp until it has bonded.

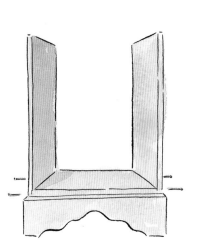

3 Fit the base piece inside, and position it so the top sits level with the top of the pedestal. Glue and nail through the sides to hold it in place.

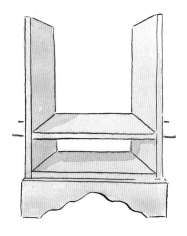

4 Mark a line 3 inches above the base and fix the bottom edge of the shelf level with the line. Glue and nail through from the sides as before.

5 To make up the dividing framework for the small drawers, the vertical and horizontal dividers are slotted together. Dribble some glue where the dividers are to be joined and push the sections into one another to form the frame. Make sure that the framework remains true and square. Then glue the side and bottom edges and slot the framework into the chest carcase from the front.

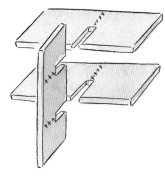

TOOLS AND EQUIPMENT

tracing paper and pencil
clamps
coping saw and tenon saw
medium and fine sandpaper
wood glue
finishing nails and hammer
ruler
router or ⅛-inch chisel and mallet
bradawl
screwdriver

PAINT SWATCHES

Brown-red
I part Indian red
3 parts water-based
varnish

Golden yellow
I part yellow ochre
I part burnt umber
3 parts water-based
varnish

PAINT PALETTE AND EQUIPMENT

white acrylic primer
artists' acrylic paints in the following
colors:
Indian red
yellow ochre
burnt umber
water-based satin varnish
shallow white container, for mixing
¼-inch square-tipped artists' brush
No. 5 lining brush
soft varnishing brush

6 Place the top section in position, nailing down into the sides and vertical divider. Apply glue to the bottom edge of the pediment and position it centrally, flush with the front edge. Clamp in place until the glue has bonded.

7 Fit the back onto the main body of the chest and glue and nail it in place around the edges and along the line of the vertical divider.

8 Glue and nail the top trim, using the short sections for the sides and the longer one for the front; make sure they are flush with the top edge. Repeat for the bottom, positioning the top of all the sections level with the base and the top of the pedestal.

9 To assemble the drawers, use a router to make a rabbet ⅜ inch wide by ⅛ inch deep down both sides of the drawer front on the inside. Alternatively, use a chisel and mallet, cutting along the scored lines with a saw to the correct depth before removing the waste wood. Glue the sides into the rabbets. Glue the back piece and butt it up to the sides. Cut the base to fit and glue it inside the frame, flush with the bottom edges. Reinforce the joints by nailing through from the sides.

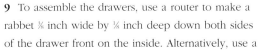

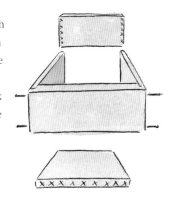

10 To finish, make pilot holes in the middle of each drawer with a bradawl and screw in the knobs.

STEPS TO PAINT

1 Prime the drawers with white acrylic primer and allow to dry. Rub smooth with fine sandpaper.

2 Make up the golden yellow color for the drawers and apply to the fronts of each. Use different brush-strokes to imitate wood grain. Experiment with different effects so you get a variety of patterns. Use the ¼-inch square-tipped brush for the main pattern and the No. 5 lining brush to add dots and details. This type of wood graining is not expected to reproduce any particular grain—it is more impressionistic.

3 Make up the brown-red color by tinting the clear varnish with Indian red, as listed, then paint the frame. Let dry.

4 Darken this mixture with extra Indian red, then, using the No. 5 lining brush, add the outlines on the frame and paint the knobs. Let dry.

5 Apply at least one coat of satin varnish and allow to dry. If adding further coats of varnish, smooth the spice chest with fine sandpaper between coats.

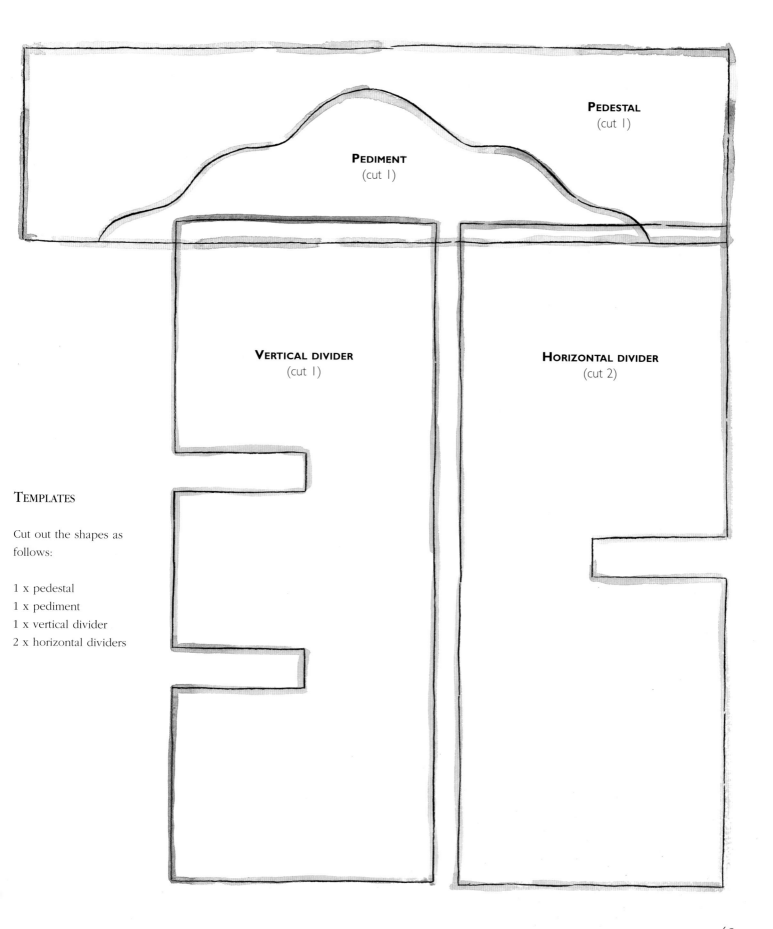

PEDESTAL
(cut 1)

PEDIMENT
(cut 1)

VERTICAL DIVIDER
(cut 1)

HORIZONTAL DIVIDER
(cut 2)

TEMPLATES

Cut out the shapes as
follows:

1 x pedestal
1 x pediment
1 x vertical divider
2 x horizontal dividers

KEY CUPBOARD

Finding keys can become a permanent pastime unless you always return them to the same place. This shallow cupboard has been designed so that you will never need to search for keys again.

1 Butt the edges of the side panels up to the back piece and glue as shown. Reinforce with finishing nails knocked in from the back.

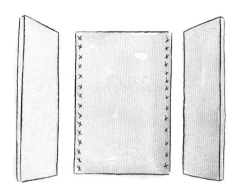

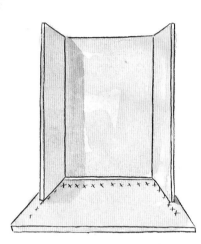

2 Apply glue to the underside of the assembled back and sides and attach them to the base; position the base so that one long edge is flush with the back of the side panels, leaving an equal ⅜-inch overhang at both sides.

3 Apply glue to the top of the assembled cupboard and position the top section so that it corresponds exactly with the base—flush with the back and with a ⅜-inch overlap around the front and sides. Smooth all edges with medium, then fine, sandpaper.

4 To make the door, assemble the frame pieces as shown, apply glue, and butt the pieces together.

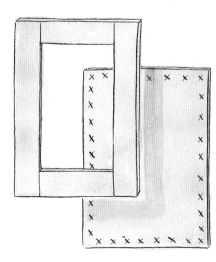

5 Apply glue to the plywood door, as shown, then lay the assembled frame on top. Press together until the glue has bonded. Smooth the joined edges with sandpaper.

MATERIALS

½-inch softwood, cut as follows:
  two 9½ x 2¼ inches, for sides
  two 8 x 2⅞ inches, for base and
    top
¼-inch softwood, cut as follows:
  two 9½ x 1¼ inches, for door
    frame sides
  two 3¾ x 1¼ inches, for door
    frame top and bottom
¼-inch plywood, cut as follows:
  one 9½ x 7¼ inches, for back
  one 9½ x 6¼ inches, for door panel
small strip of wood, 1¾-inch length,
  for door stop
small door knob (with screw)

TOOLS AND EQUIPMENT

wood glue
finishing nails
hammer
medium and fine sandpaper
bradawl
screwdriver
2 butt hinges (with screws)
8 cup hooks (with screws), for keys
hand drill, with ⅛-inch screw bit

51

6 Next attach the door knob; the one used here has a diameter of ¾ inch. Make a pilot hole for the knob, using a bradawl, and screw it in place halfway down the right-hand frame.

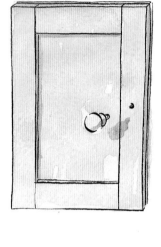

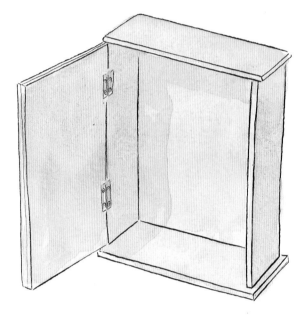

7 Position hinges on the inside of the door as shown. Make pilot holes for the screws with a bradawl and screw the hinges in position. Check that the door closes properly without rubbing; adjust the tightness of the screws if necessary to make sure that the door hangs evenly.

8 Stick a small piece of wood to the top inside of the right-hand panel, ½ inch in from the front, so that the door will close to the correct position.

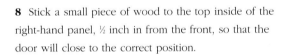

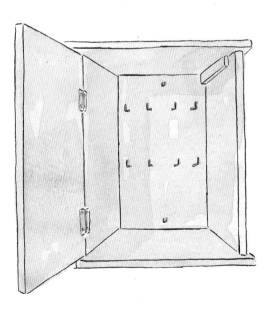

9 Using a bradawl, make pilot holes for the hooks. Position the hooks in two neat rows of four, with a gap in between to allow the keys to hang down. Screw the hooks in place. Mark two more holes through the entire thickness of the wood at the top and bottom of the rear panel for securing the cupboard to a wall. Use a hand drill fitted with a ⅛-inch screw bit to drill the holes.

PAINT PALETTE AND EQUIPMENT

cream latex paint

blue-gray latex paint

water-based satin varnish

medium household paintbrush

pencil

tracing paper

¼-inch soft artists' brush

soft cloth

square-tipped varnishing brush

STEPS TO PAINT

1 Using a household paintbrush, paint the cupboard with a base coat of cream latex paint, and let dry.

2 Apply a top coat of blue-gray latex paint.

3 Mark out a border lightly in pencil ½ inch inside the central door panel.

4 Trace the key pattern (opposite). Rub the back of the tracing with a soft pencil, then transfer it onto the wood by placing it on the center of the panel and going over the outline. Make all the pencil markings very light.

5 Use the ¼-inch brush and the cream latex paint to draw a ¼-inch border around the central panel, working inside your pencil guideline.

6 Color in the key using the same brush and cream paint as was used for the border. Allow to dry completely.

7 Using the medium sandpaper, rub back the paint all over the cupboard, always following the direction of the wood grain as you do so. In the same way, remove some of the paint on the edges and corners for a naturally worn, aged look.

8 Dust the cupboard well before applying the water-based satin varnish with a clean square-tipped brush. If necessary, apply a further coat of varnish, but make sure the first coat is completely dry before doing so.

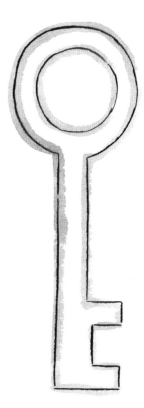

TEMPLATE

Trace the template as follows:

1 x key motif

WOODEN TRAY

This very simple rectangular wooden tray has been given a Japanese feel by painting a dark orange pattern on a black background and varnishing it to a high sheen. The tray itself is not difficult to make—the planing of the beveled edge is the only challenging part.

YOU WILL NEED

MATERIALS

¼-inch plywood, 18 x 12 inches, for
  base
1-x-1½-inch softwood, 68-inch
  length, for sides

TOOLS AND EQUIPMENT

miter box
tenon saw
pencil
ruler
clamps
plane
medium and fine sandpaper
wood glue
finishing nails
hammer

PAINT PALETTE AND EQUIPMENT

black latex paint
artists' acrylic paints in the following
  colors:
    cadmium orange
    cadmium red deep
clear water-based satin varnish
shallow white container, for mixing
broad household paintbrush
piece of chalk
artists' brushes, Nos. 2 and 5
1-inch square-tipped varnishing brush
soft cloth

1 Using a miter box and tenon saw, miter the ends of the
four side pieces at 45°, so that they fit together on top of
the base. After mitering, the lengths should be 18 inches
for the long sides and 12 inches for the short sides.

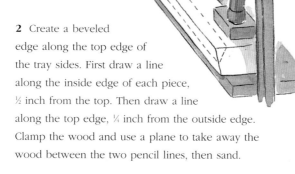

2 Create a beveled
edge along the top edge of
the tray sides. First draw a line
along the inside edge of each piece,
½ inch from the top. Then draw a line
along the top edge, ¼ inch from the outside edge.
Clamp the wood and use a plane to take away the
wood between the two pencil lines, then sand.

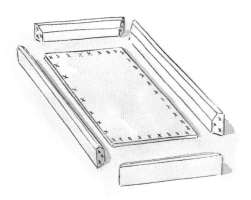

3 To assemble the tray, start by gluing the four side
pieces together at the corners to create a frame. Then
place the frame on top of the base and glue in place.
Strengthen the joints by tapping finishing nails across
the corners and up through the base.

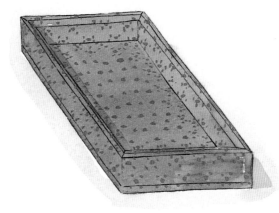

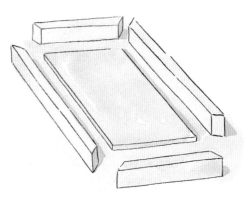

PAINT SWATCH

Dark orange
  3 parts cadmium orange
  1 part cadmium red deep

STEPS TO PAINT

1 Start by painting the entire tray with two
coats of black latex paint, using a broad
household paintbrush. Let dry.

2 Use a piece of chalk to mark out a
central panel for the decoration, measuring
13 x 7 inches.

3 Mix up three parts cadmium orange to
one part cadmium red deep. Then use the
No. 5 brush to cover the central panel with
even rows of dots.

4 Using the No. 2 brush, paint rows of the
five-dot motif, in the same colored paint,
around the edge of the central panel and
over the sides until the tray is completely
covered. Allow the paint to dry.

5 Apply a coat of varnish with a square-
tipped brush. Allow to dry, then sand
lightly with medium and fine sandpaper.
Dust well before applying another coat of
varnish. Keep on varnishing and sanding;
the more coats of varnish you apply, the
better the tray will look.

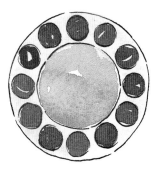

YOU WILL NEED

MATERIALS, TOOLS, AND EQUIPMENT

sufficient ½-inch laminated pine or
   plywood to cut the following piece:
   one 8-inch-diameter circle (or larger
   or smaller as required)

tracing paper

pencil

compass

clamps

saber saw or coping saw

medium and fine sandpaper

soft cloth

scrap wood

drill

quartz clock movement

PAINT PALETTE AND EQUIPMENT

white acrylic primer

artists' acrylic paints in the following
   colors:
   golden ochre
   white
   cadmium red deep
   vermilion
   sap green
   brilliant blue

water

water-based satin varnish

shallow white container, for mixing

household paintbrush

protractor

stencil cardboard or sheet of clear
   plastic

craft knife

No. 3 artists' brush

½-inch square-tipped artists' brush

varnishing brush

CLOCK FACE

*To make the clock, simply cut a circle out of wood, sand the edges smooth
and drill a hole for the movement. The design can either be traced or
drawn freehand and the shapes filled in with different colors.*

1 To make the clock the same size as the template on page 59, trace the design and, at first, transfer the outer ring only onto the wood.

   If you want a larger or smaller clock, either alter the size of the template accordingly on a photocopier and then trace off the outer circle as above, or draw the clock freehand by setting the compass to your chosen radius and drawing the outer circle.

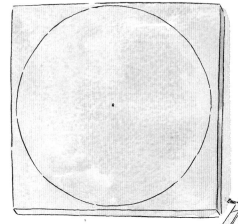

2 Using clamps, attach the wood to a tabletop or workbench and cut out the circle with a saber saw or coping saw. Sand the edges with medium and fine sandpaper, then dust well before painting.

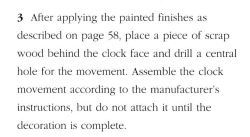

3 After applying the painted finishes as described on page 58, place a piece of scrap wood behind the clock face and drill a central hole for the movement. Assemble the clock movement according to the manufacturer's instructions, but do not attach it until the decoration is complete.

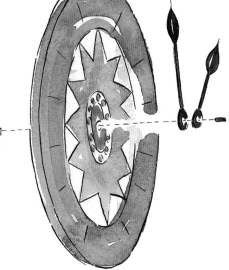

PAINT SWATCHES

Yellow
2 parts golden ochre
1 part white

Red
2 parts cadmium red deep
1 part vermilion

Green-blue
1 part sap green
1 part brilliant blue

STEPS TO PAINT

1 Using a household paintbrush, prime the wood with white acrylic primer and allow to dry.

2 Make up the yellow color for the background by mixing golden ochre and white. Paint this onto the clock face as a base coat.

3 If you have decided to trace the template, either having altered its size or not, take your tracing and position it carefully over your circle of wood. Then transfer the inner circles, numbers, and star shape onto the painted wood.

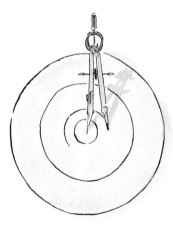

4 If you are drawing the design freehand, first use a compass to draw a circle for the outer ring, then draw the two inner rings to the correct proportions, using the template as a rough guide. Use a protractor to divide the outer ring into 12 equal segments and carefully draw all the numerals in position in the segments.

5 Complete the planning of the clock face by drawing in the dots inside the inner ring; you can use a small circular stencil for this, or you can cut your own from cardboard or a sheet of clear plastic. Finally, draw the star shape.

6 Mix up the red paint by adding vermilion to cadmium red deep and thin the paint slightly with water so that it flows well. Use a No. 3 artists' brush to outline the numerals and fill in the background of the outer ring; the yellow base coat acts as the color for the numbers.

7 Make up the green-blue by mixing equal parts of sap green and brilliant blue. Use this color to paint the star shape with a ¼-inch square-tipped brush.

8 Paint the dots of the inner ring in red.

9 To finish the decoration, use the No. 3 brush and the green-blue paint to mark the segments between the numerals.

10 Apply a coat of satin varnish and leave to dry. Sand with fine sandpaper, then varnish again. Repeat at least four times to give a smooth, shiny surface. Finally, attach the clock mechanism.

TEMPLATE

Enlarge or reduce the template
on a photocopier, if preferred,
and cut out the shape as follows:

1 x clock face

59

The Playroom

PULL-ALONG DUCK

Small children love simple wooden toys that are designed to be pulled along. This little white duck is made from reclaimed floorboards, well sanded to a smooth but interestingly grained surface. Once the toy phase has passed, the duck can be recycled as an ornament.

YOU WILL NEED

MATERIALS

sufficient ½-inch reclaimed wood,
   such as floorboards, to cut the
   following pieces:
   one 5⅛ x 7⅜ inches, for body and
      head
   one 6¹¹⁄₁₆ x 3⅜ inches, for base
   two 2¼ x 3⅜ inches, for wings
   four 1¾-inch-diameter circles, for
      wheels
2 wooden buttons with back
   loops, for eyes
1 large wooden bead, for cord
¼-inch wooden doweling, 12-inch
   length, for axle dowels
⅛-inch wooden doweling, 6-inch
   length, for wing and wheel dowels
thick twine, 40 inches

TOOLS AND EQUIPMENT

tracing paper
pencil
clamps
saber saw
drill, with ¼-inch and ⅛-inch twist
   bits (see Beginner's Tip, below)
medium and fine sandpaper
sanding block (optional)
scrap wood
ruler
wood glue
hammer
elastic thread, 4 inches
2-inch No. 10 wood screw
screwdriver

BEGINNER'S TIP

It is easier to drill very fine holes
with a hand drill, since small bits
may snap under pressure.

1 Trace all the pattern shapes on page 65 and transfer them onto the reclaimed floorboards. Remember to include all the X marks, which show where the eyes, twine, and body of the duck are attached.

2 With clamps, attach the wood firmly to a tabletop or workbench. Use a saber saw to cut out all the shapes. Then, using a drill fitted with a ¼-inch bit, make holes through each of the wheels to take the axle dowels.

3 Sand each of the shapes with medium and then fine sandpaper, rounding off all the corners and edges to achieve a smooth finish ready for painting. When sanding the flat surfaces, you may find it helpful to wrap the sandpaper around a sanding block.

4 Make four X marks on the edges of the longest sides of the base, 1¼ inches in from the ends. Holding the base secure with clamps, drill four axle holes through the X marks 1¼ inches into the base to fit the ¼-inch dowels.

5 Place a piece of scrap wood underneath the duck's body to protect your work surface and secure both pieces to the bench with clamps. Using a ⅛-inch bit, drill holes at the X mark through the head for the eyes, and through the center of the body for the wings. Drill similar holes halfway through the thickness of the wings, on the inside.

   The pieces should now be painted before assembly (see step 6, page 64).

6 Paint all the shapes with one coat of white acrylic primer, then leave to dry for an hour. When dry, rub back with sandpaper to allow some of the grain to show through. Paint the base and the buttons for the eyes blue. Paint the wheels, beak and bead with cadmium orange. When dry, sand back each of the painted pieces to reveal some of the grain.

7 Measure and cut a piece of the ⅛-inch doweling to fit through the body and halfway into each wing. Apply a small drop of glue to the drilled hole in the body, then carefully tap the dowel through with a hammer. Tap the wings onto the dowels so they fit snugly.

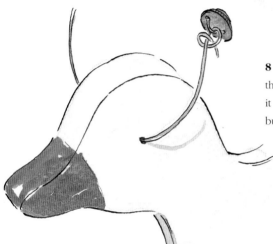

8 To make the eyes, secure the elastic thread to the back loop of one button, then thread the elastic through the hole in the head. Stretch the elastic, thread it onto the second button and secure with a firm knot. Apply glue to both button backs and release the elastic to hold the buttons firmly in place.

9 To make the axle dowels, cut the ¼-inch doweling into four 2½-inch lengths, so that they fit into the axle holes in the base and through a wheel, leaving ¾ inch of dowel extending beyond each wheel. Paint them blue and allow to dry, then drill a ⅛-inch hole ¼–½ inch from one end of each piece to take the wheel dowels. Apply a little glue to the other end of each axle dowel, then tap them through the axle holes with a hammer. Put a wheel on the end of each. To make the wheel dowels, cut the remaining ⅛-inch doweling into four ⅜-inch lengths and coat with blue paint. When they are completely dry, insert one in each of the axle dowels to hold the wheels.

10 To secure the duck to the base, drill a hole up through the base, as marked. Then drill a smaller hole in the bottom of the duck to take the screw. Attach the base to the duck, using the large wood screw.

11 Drill a hole through the front of the base, as marked, to take the twine. Tie a knot in one end of the twine, thread the cord through the hole, then through the large bead. Tie a second knot at the other end of the twine to secure the bead.

PAINT PALETTE AND EQUIPMENT

white acrylic primer

artists' acrylic paints in the following colors:

brilliant blue

white

cadmium orange

shallow white container, for mixing

⅜-inch artists' brush

PAINT SWATCHES

Blue

3 parts brilliant blue
1 part white

Cadmium orange

TEMPLATES

Cut out the shapes as follows:

1 x body and head
2 x wings
1 x base
4 x wheels

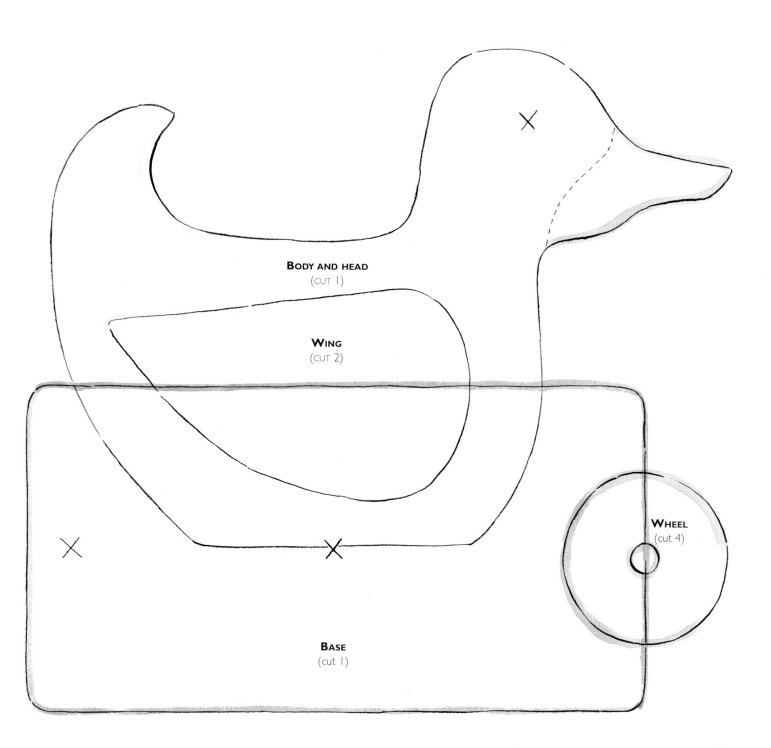

BODY AND HEAD
(CUT 1)

WING
(CUT 2)

WHEEL
(cut 4)

BASE
(cut 1)

65

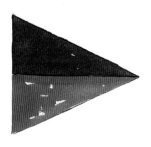

GAMES BOARD

This style of checkerboard—with the checks in the middle and sections at each end for keeping the pieces—can be found in many American folk museums, with designs stenciled or hand painted with great individuality.

YOU WILL NEED

MATERIALS

¼-inch plywood, 20 x 12½ inches, for base
¼-x-1¼-inch softwood, cut as follows:
  two 20-inch lengths, for sides
  two 12-inch lengths, for ends
  two 12-inch lengths, for dividers

TOOLS AND EQUIPMENT

wood glue
finishing nails
hammer
ruler
pencil
medium and fine sandpaper

PAINT PALETTE AND EQUIPMENT

white acrylic primer
black latex paint
artists' acrylic paints in the following
  colors:
    sap green
    brilliant blue
    golden ochre
    cadmium orange
    cadmium red deep
    cadmium scarlet
    Venetian red
    red violet
water-based satin varnish
shallow white container, for mixing
household paintbrush
strip of cardboard, 1½ x 12 inches
¼-inch square-tipped artists' brush
No. 5 artists' brush
varnishing brush

1 Assemble the outside frame of the board on top of the base. The shorter end lengths butt up to the longer side pieces. Glue along all adjoining surfaces, then reinforce with finishing nails.

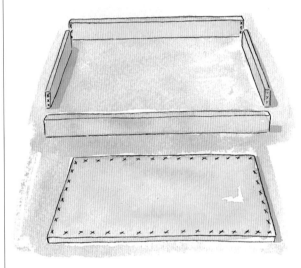

2 Measure 3½ inches from each end piece and mark parallel lines on the base. Glue the two dividers centrally onto this line, so that the spaces at each end measure 3½ x 12 inches and the middle square is 12 x 12 inches. Reinforce with finishing nails inserted from underneath.

Before painting the design (see below), sand all the rough edges for a smooth finish.

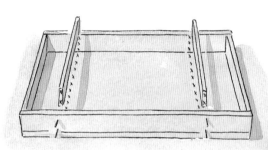

STEPS TO PAINT

1 Use a household paintbrush to paint the games board (inside and out) with white acrylic primer. Allow to dry.

2 Using the strip of cardboard or a ruler as a guide, draw the checkerboard plan on the central panel. There are eight 1½-x-1½-inch squares along each edge. Carefully fill in every alternate square with black latex paint, using a ¼-inch square-tipped brush.

3 With a pencil, divide the end panels in half vertically, then in half again horizontally. Draw intersecting diagonals across the two halves.

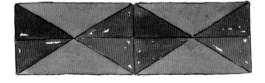

4 Use a No. 5 brush to paint the end panels in the colors shown opposite, top right, and leave to dry.

5 Paint the inside edges of the sides and the top rim in bright red. When dry, paint the outside edges and the base with black latex paint. Allow to dry overnight, then seal with water-based satin varnish.

PAINT SWATCHES

Green
 1 part sap green
 1 part brilliant blue

Orange
 1 part golden ochre
 1 part cadmium orange

Bright red
 1 part cadmium red deep
 1 part cadmium scarlet

Dark red
 3 parts Venetian red
 1 part red violet

YOU WILL NEED

MATERIALS

shop-bought pencil box
¾-inch wooden doweling, 6¼-inch
   length, for pencil

TOOLS AND EQUIPMENT

tenon saw
craft knife
medium and fine sandpaper
ruler
hand drill and bit
bradawl
2 short wood screws
screwdriver

PAINT PALETTE AND EQUIPMENT

white acrylic primer
gray-green latex paint
artists' acrylic paints in the following
   colors:
   deep brilliant red (or any other
     primary color)
   hooker's green
   raw umber
   white
water-based satin varnish
shallow white container, for mixing
small household paintbrush
strip of cardboard, ⅛-inch wide
¼-inch and ⅛-inch square-tipped
   artists' brushes

PAINT SWATCHES

Hooker's green

Raw umber

Deep brilliant red

PENCIL BOX

This is a standard, store-bought wooden pencil box with a sliding lid—the sort that has been around ever since children first owned pencils. The decorative pencil on top is made from wooden doweling, sharpened to a point at one end.

1 Using a tenon saw, cut the doweling to fit the lid of the pencil box. Sharpen one end using a sharp craft knife.

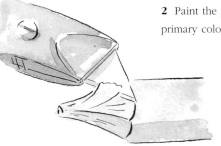

2 Paint the pencil shaft and the sharpened "lead" in red (or another primary color). Apply a coat of water-based satin varnish and let dry.

3 Sand the pencil box to provide a surface for keying the paint, then apply a base coat of gray-green latex paint.

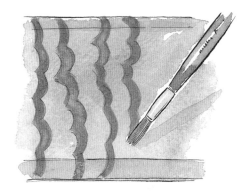

4 The pattern looks like pencil shavings. Use the strip of cardboard to keep your rows more or less parallel and ⅜ inch apart. Practice the brushstroke before you begin. Dilute the hooker's green with water so that it flows well, and use the ¼-inch square-tipped brush to paint even rows of scallops.

5 Mix a dash of raw umber into some white paint and use the thinner ⅛-inch square-tipped brush to paint rows of scallops in between the others. Make sure you leave some background color showing through.

6 Drill two holes through the lid (about 2½ inches apart) and make two small corresponding pilot holes in the "pencil" with a bradawl. Screw the pencil to the lid from underneath.

7 Seal the box with one or two coats of water-based satin varnish, smoothing with fine sandpaper between coats.

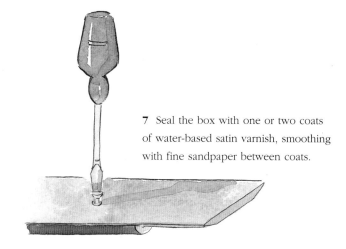

CLOWN PUPPET

Balsa is quite different from any other type of wood. It is extremely lightweight and has no obvious grain, so it can be sanded easily and requires no drilling—you simply pierce holes through the wood using a bradawl.

1 To make the upper torso, take four equal-sized cubes of balsa and join them together with wood glue to form a block approximately 3 inches high. Clamp or tape them together overnight to bond the glue. Make up the lower torso in the same way.

2 Trim away the sides of the assembled blocks with a craft knife to shape the upper and lower torsos, then smooth with sandpaper, taking care not to sand away too much at once. Both have an approximate circumference of 6 inches tapering to 5 inches. Shape the wood for the arms and legs in the same way; each of the four pieces for the arms is approximately 1¾ inches long, and each leg piece is approximately 2 inches long. Cut two small wedge-shaped pieces for the shoulders. Shape the head with a flat top and a round base from a cube of wood approximately 1½ inches square (two wheels and a button fit on top to make the hat, so use these as a guide for shaping the crown of the head).

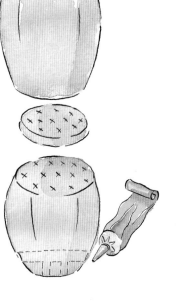

3 To assemble the clown's body, glue the largest wooden wheel between the shaped upper and lower torsos. Using a bradawl, pierce two holes ¾ inch deep into the base of the lower torso to take the legs. Make a hole across the lower torso from one side to the other to intersect these two holes. Fill the entrances of the side holes with wood filler, leaving the inside channel free for threading on the legs. Before assembling the rest of the puppet, paint the wood following the steps on page 72.

YOU WILL NEED

MATERIALS

pack of assorted balsa wood
  (available in various shapes and
  sizes, both square and round—
  cubes are used here)
wooden wheels, 1 large, 1 medium,
  and 1 small (approximately
  1½ inches, 1 inch, and ½ inch in
  diameter; available from model
  stores)
1 button with metal-looped back
11 colored wooden beads
¼-x-½-inch softwood, two 6-inch
  lengths, for crossbars

TOOLS AND EQUIPMENT

wood glue
clamps or masking tape
craft knife
medium and fine sandpaper
bradawl
wood filler
plastic-coated wire, 6 inches
elastic thread and needle
paper fastener

PAINT PALETTE AND EQUIPMENT

white acrylic primer
artists' acrylic paints in the following
   colors:
   white
   cadmium red
   brilliant blue
   hooker's green
   cadmium yellow
water-based satin varnish
shallow white container,
   for mixing
½-inch artists' brush
No. 1 artists' brush
square-tipped varnishing
   brush

PAINT SWATCHES

White

Cadmium red

Brilliant blue

Hooker's green

Cadmium yellow

STEPS TO PAINT

1 Start by applying a base coat of white acrylic primer to all the pieces. Allow to dry for 1 hour, then follow with a coat of the selected color for each part, as indicated on the left. Use the No. 1 artists' brush to paint the facial features. Let dry.

2 Use a square-tipped brush to apply a water-based satin varnish to all the pieces and allow to dry overnight before assembly.

STEPS TO ASSEMBLE

1 Using a bradawl, pierce all the shaped balsa components for the arms and legs lengthwise. Then make a hole from top to bottom through the middle of the head.

2 Begin by assembling the head. Push a length of wire through the button back to make a small loop, then twist the wire around itself to secure it. Thread the small and then the medium wheel onto the wire to make up the hat. Then thread the wire through the hole in the head and, finally, through the bead for the neck.

3 Using a bradawl, make a central hole 1¼ inches deep in the top of the upper torso for attaching the head to the body. Then make another intersecting hole across the upper torso to support and attach the arms; it should intersect the vertical neck hole about ¼ inch above the base of the hole.

   Make a loop at least 1¼ inches long at the end of the wire that supports the head, so that it fits inside the neck hole. Twist the loose end around itself to secure it, then feed it back inside the neck bead to neaten. When the arms are attached, the elastic on which they are threaded will pass through the wire neck loop to secure the head.

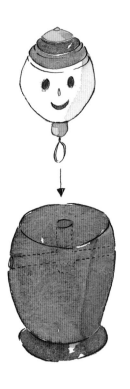

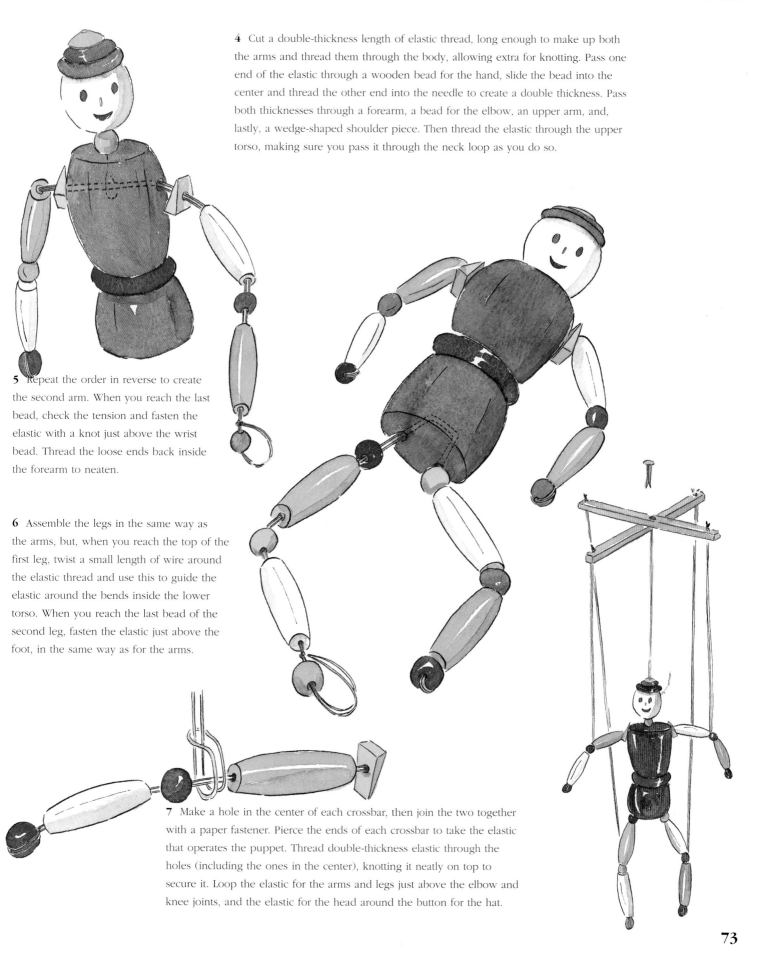

4 Cut a double-thickness length of elastic thread, long enough to make up both the arms and thread them through the body, allowing extra for knotting. Pass one end of the elastic through a wooden bead for the hand, slide the bead into the center and thread the other end into the needle to create a double thickness. Pass both thicknesses through a forearm, a bead for the elbow, an upper arm, and, lastly, a wedge-shaped shoulder piece. Then thread the elastic through the upper torso, making sure you pass it through the neck loop as you do so.

5 Repeat the order in reverse to create the second arm. When you reach the last bead, check the tension and fasten the elastic with a knot just above the wrist bead. Thread the loose ends back inside the forearm to neaten.

6 Assemble the legs in the same way as the arms, but, when you reach the top of the first leg, twist a small length of wire around the elastic thread and use this to guide the elastic around the bends inside the lower torso. When you reach the last bead of the second leg, fasten the elastic just above the foot, in the same way as for the arms.

7 Make a hole in the center of each crossbar, then join the two together with a paper fastener. Pierce the ends of each crossbar to take the elastic that operates the puppet. Thread double-thickness elastic through the holes (including the ones in the center), knotting it neatly on top to secure it. Loop the elastic for the arms and legs just above the elbow and knee joints, and the elastic for the head around the button for the hat.

POP-UP TOY

Make this simple toy for a toddler and enjoy the reaction it gets. It combines two things that really appeal to the very young—control and surprise! The toy is made from two identical pieces of plywood that sandwich the little character inside. As the lever is moved, it pops up out of the tree.

YOU WILL NEED

MATERIALS

sufficient ¼-inch plywood for the
following pieces:

two 3¾ x 3⅛ inches, for front and
back

one 3 x ³⁄₁₆ inch, for lever

one 2⅞ x 1⅝ inches, for figure

sufficient ½-inch softwood to cut the
following pieces:

two 3¹⁵⁄₁₆ x ⅝ inch, for sides

¼-inch wooden doweling, two small
lengths, for hinging lever and figure

TOOLS AND EQUIPMENT

tracing paper

pencil

clamps or vise

coping saw

tenon saw

medium and fine sandpaper

scrap wood

hand drill, with ¼-inch screw bit

wood glue

craft knife

1¼-inch chisel

mallet

finishing nails

hammer

1 Trace the templates on page 77 and transfer them onto the wood. Clamp the wood to a workbench and cut out the shapes using a coping saw for curved edges and a tenon saw for straight ends, then sand the rough edges.

2 Drill a hole in the front piece to insert the blade of the coping saw. Then clamp and cut out the window shape.

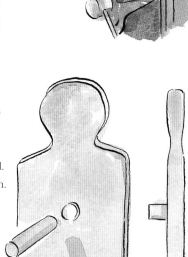

3 Cut the elongated hole out of the lever, clamping the wood and using the coping saw as before.

4 Place a piece of scrap wood behind the figure and drill a ¼-inch hole where marked to fit the wooden dowel. Glue it in place, then sand the front so that the dowel is flush with the plywood. Trim the back of the dowel to protrude by ⅛ inch.

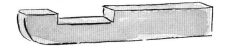

5 Use a craft knife to score two parallel lines in one of the side pieces, as marked by the dotted lines on the template. Saw along the scored lines to a depth of ¼ inch, then use a chisel and mallet to hollow out the waste wood in between.

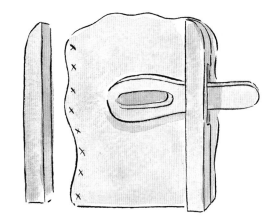

6 Glue the side pieces onto the back, placing the recessed piece face-down on the right-hand side. Insert the lever so that it protrudes through the hole.

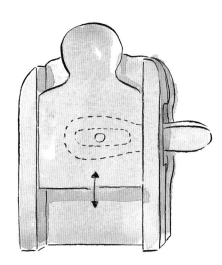

7 Place the figure over the lever with the dowel going through the elongated hole. Move the lever up and down to gauge the position for the lever fixing. Sand the edges as necessary until the figure has free movement up and down.

PAINT PALETTE AND EQUIPMENT

white acrylic primer
artists' acrylic paints in the
 following colors:
 brown
 vermilion
 light yellow
 black
 hooker's green
 white
 bright red
water-based satin varnish (safe for
 children's toys)
shallow white container, for mixing
broad artists' brush
No. 1 artists' brush
No. 4 artists' brush
varnishing brush

PAINT SWATCHES

Vermilion

Bright red

Cadmium yellow

Light yellow

Hooker's green

Light green
 1 part hooker's green
 1 part white

Black

Brown

Blue-green
 3 parts ultramarine
 1 part cadmium yellow

Bright blue

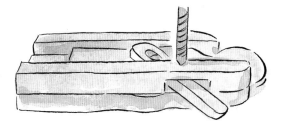

8 Drill a ¼-inch hole through the side, lever, and back, then glue and insert a dowel. Trim and sand it front and back until it is flush with the plywood.

9 Paint the lever in brown and, when it has dried completely, apply a coat of varnish.

10 Put the front panel in place to check that the movement works smoothly. If it does not, sand the edges of all the moving parts until free movement is gained. Leave the final assembly until after the figure has been painted.

STEPS TO PAINT

1 Paint all pieces in white acrylic primer and leave to dry. Paint the figure's clothing in vermilion and the hair in light yellow. Then, using the No. 1 brush, paint the facial features black.

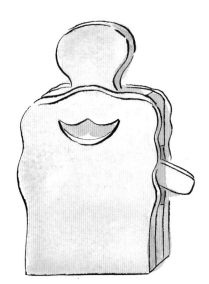

2 Next, paint the front, back and sides light green. When this has dried, add the apples in bright red and the leaves in hooker's green. To finish, seal all the painted pieces with a coat of water-based satin varnish; choose a brand that is safe for use on children's toys.

TO ASSEMBLE

1 Assemble the toy by gluing the front to the sides. If necessary, strengthen with small finishing nails inserted through the back into the sides.

PAINT PALETTE FOR ALTERNATIVE DESIGN

white acrylic primer

artists' acrylic paints in the following colors:

brown

light yellow

bright blue

black

ultramarine

cadmium yellow

hooker's green

ALTERNATIVE DESIGN

The alternative toy is painted blue-green and the figure is dressed in bright blue. The apples are replaced with yellow pears.

1 As before, paint the lever brown and the hair light yellow. Paint the figure's clothing in bright blue. Then add the facial features in black with the No. 1 brush.

2 Paint the front, back, and sides blue-green. Add the leaves in hooker's green. When completely dry, paint the pears cadmium yellow and their stalks brown.

3 Leave the paint to dry completely before varnishing and assembly (see opposite page).

TEMPLATES

Cut out the shapes as follows:

1 x lever

1 x figure

2 x front and back

2 x sides

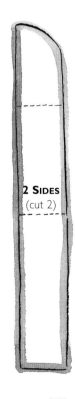

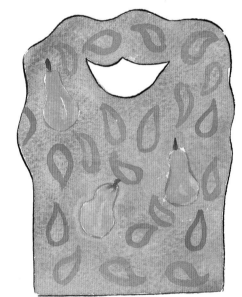

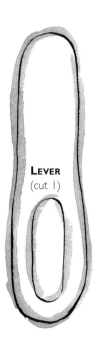

LEVER
(cut 1)

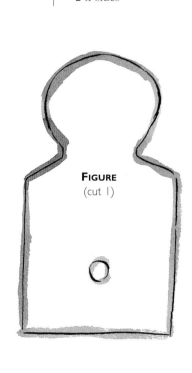

FIGURE
(cut 1)

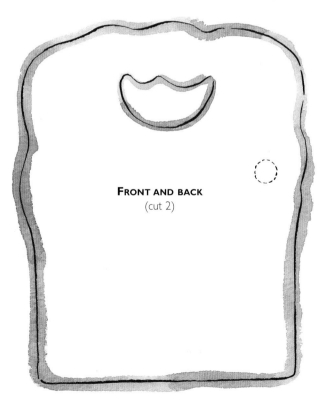

FRONT AND BACK
(cut 2)

2 SIDES
(cut 2)

PEG RAIL

The simple shape and construction of this peg rail make it an ideal project for someone who is fond of painting but has a limited number of tools. The size of the board and the number of pegs can be adjusted to suit your needs.

YOU WILL NEED

MATERIALS

1-x-6-inch softwood, 30-inch length

¾-inch wooden doweling, four
  16-inch lengths, for pegs

TOOLS AND EQUIPMENT

handsaw

medium and fine sandpaper

pencil

ruler

drill, with ½-inch screw bit

craft knife

wood glue

PAINT PALETTE AND EQUIPMENT

white acrylic primer

yellow latex paint

artists' acrylic paints in the following
  colors:
  sap green
  yellow ochre
  cadmium yellow
  alizarin crimson
  cobalt blue
  raw umber
  dioxazine purple
  white

water-based satin varnish

tracing paper

medium household paintbrush

No. 4 artists' brush

fine lining brush

varnishing brush

1 Using a handsaw, cut away a triangular piece of wood 1¾ inches deep from the top corners of the softwood to give the shape of the peg rail. Sand all the cut edges to give a smooth, slightly beveled appearance.

2 Mark out four holes for the pegs on the front of the peg rail, positioning them 1¾ inches from the bottom edge. The holes at either end should be placed 4¼ inches from the edge and the others should be 6½ inches apart. Fit the drill with a ½-inch bit and drill out the holes to a depth of ¾ inch.

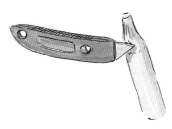

3 Using a craft knife, carve one end of the dowel pegs to fit snugly into the ½-inch holes. Roughen up the sides and ends of the pegs with medium sandpaper so that they look more like whittled wood than machined dowels. Paint the board and pegs (see below), allow the varnish to dry completely, then glue the pegs into the holes.

PAINT SWATCHES

Sap green	Cadmium yellow	Raw umber
Yellow ochre	Alizarin crimson	Dioxazine purple
	Cobalt blue	White

STEPS TO PAINT

1 Using a medium household paintbrush, prime the entire peg rail with white acrylic primer and leave it to dry before painting a base coat of yellow latex paint. Using tracing paper and a pencil, trace the basic shapes that you intend to use on page 79 and transfer them onto the wood.

2 Start by painting the backgrounds of the houses in different colors, then add the larger details, such as the roofs, steeples, and domes. Either choose your own colors or use the templates as guides.

3 Use a fine lining brush to add the windows, doorways, and detailing on the trees in your chosen colors. Allow the paint to dry after each stage so that you don't smudge the edges.

4 Paint the dowel pegs to match the main background color, then fit them into the holes, as shown in step 3, above.

5 When you are satisfied with the overall look, apply at least two coats of varnish to the entire rail.

TEMPLATES

Enlarge the template on a photocopier, if preferred, and trace the basic shapes you wish to use.

MONEY BOX

This money box looks so authentically old that it is practically a fake! The construction is simple but satisfying with scope for some fine detail—such as the cutting of the money slot and the beveling of the top edges.

YOU WILL NEED

MATERIALS

¾-inch softwood, cut as follows:
  two 5 x 3½ inches, for sides
  two 5 x 9 inches, for front
    and back
  one 9½ x 5½ inches, for top
  one approximately 7½ x 3½ inches,
    for base (cut to fit)
approximately ½-x-½-inch half-astragal
  molding, 35-inch length, to
  surround base
⅛-inch plywood, 2 x 3½ inches, to
  cover access slot

TOOLS AND EQUIPMENT

pencil
ruler
try square
scrap wood
clamps or vise
hand drill
saber saw or coping saw
medium and fine sandpaper
wood glue
finishing nails
hammer
tenon saw
plane or medium half-round file
miter box
2 wood screws
screwdriver

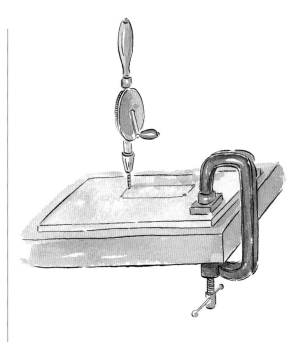

2 Next, mark out the slot for inserting the money. Draw it in the center of the top section, measuring ⅜ x 2½ inches with rounded corners. To cut out the slot, drill a hole in each corner first to create the rounded corners, protecting your work surface with scrap wood, as in step 1. Then clamp the wood in a vise or with clamps and use a coping saw to cut out the shape, inserting the blade into one of the holes. Smooth all rough edges with sandpaper.

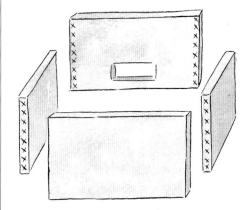

4 Cut the base to fit inside the box frame, then insert it, making sure the bottom of the base is flush with the bottom edges of the assembled sides. Glue in position and reinforce with finishing nails, inserted from the outside.

1 The slot in the back piece, which allows you access to the contents, measures 1½ x 2½ inches; use a try square to draw it ¾ inch from the bottom edge, positioning it centrally. To cut out the shape, if necessary place a piece of scrap wood under the wood to protect your work surface and clamp securely in place. First, drill a hole in one of the corners, then insert the blade of the saber saw or coping saw into the hole and cut away the wood, carefully following the pencil guideline.

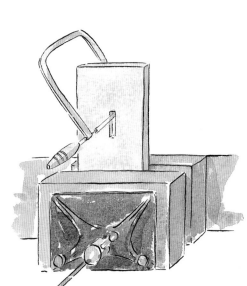

3 Assemble the four sides of the box, butting the short ends up to the front and back. Glue the edges together and then nail through from the sides to strengthen the joints.

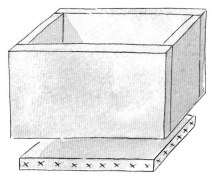

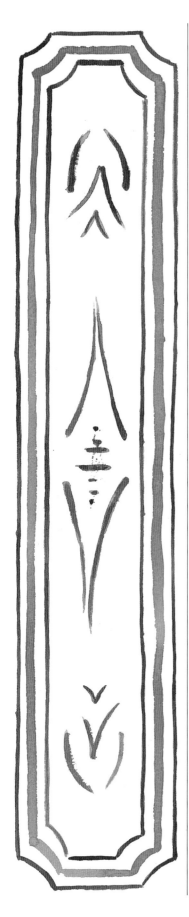

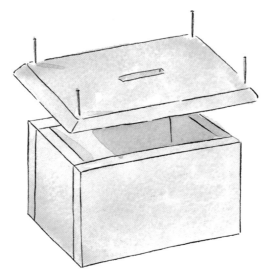

5 Before attaching the top section onto the assembled box, bevel the four edges using a plane or a file (see right), then sand them with medium and fine sandpaper to create a smooth finish.

6 Next, apply wood glue to the top edges of the front, back, and side panels. Position the top piece centrally onto the top of the box, making sure that there is an equal overhang of ¼ inch on all four sides. Finally, for additional strength, insert finishing nails through the top and into the sides in each of the four corners.

7 Take the half-astragal molding and divide it into four lengths to fit around the sides of the box. Use a miter box and tenon saw to miter both ends of each piece at an angle of 45° so that they will fit together neatly at the corner junctions. Apply wood glue around the bottom edges of the box, and glue the four pieces of molding in place, making sure that they are flush with the base so that the box will be steady.

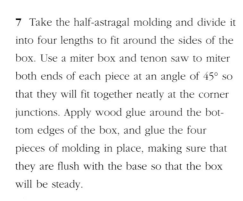

8 Clamp the plywood cover in position over the access slot, then drill two holes through the cover and the back of the box on either side of the slot. The plywood panel can now be screwed in place and easily removed when you want to get at your money! Do not screw the panel in position until the box has been painted and is thoroughly dry (see opposite), otherwise you could smudge the paintwork.

PAINT PALETTE AND EQUIPMENT

shellac

artists' oil paints in the following

  colors:

    black

    viridian green

    golden ochre

    Venetian red

    raw umber

polyurethane satin varnish

crackle glazing varnish

turpentine

dark oak antiquing varnish

shallow white container, for mixing

broad artists' brush

compass

long-bristled lining brushes, Nos. 2

  and 6

rag

soft cloth

varnishing brush

STEPS TO PAINT

1 Seal the wood with a coat of shellac. Mix the dark green background color, then apply three coats to the entire box, allowing sufficient drying time between each coat.

2 For the decoration on the front, use a compass to draw the corner curves, then draw the rest of the panel using a ruler and pencil. Repeat for the top and side panels.

3 Using the No. 6 lining brush, draw the thickest central line in golden ochre. Start on one side and save your surest strokes for the most visible part.

4 Change to the No. 2 lining brush and then paint the thinner lines in Venetian red, one on either side of the thick yellow line.

5 Finally, paint flourishes with the No. 2 lining brush in Venetian red, using any or all of the flourishes shown opposite to add an extra decorative touch. Allow to dry overnight (or for longer, if possible) before applying the varnish.

FINISHING

1 Seal the paint with a coat of polyurethane satin varnish. Then apply the crackle glazing varnish according to the manufacturer's instructions. When it is dry, put some raw umber oil paint onto a rag and rub it into the surface of the box. Leave to dry for about half an hour, then rub it off with a soft cloth dampened slightly with turpentine. Don't overdo this, or the color will lift from the cracks.

2 Apply two more coats of polyurethane varnish and allow to dry overnight before sealing the box with antiquing varnish in a dark oak shade.

3 When the varnish has dried, screw the access panel in place. Your box is now ready to use.

PAINT SWATCHES

Dark green
  3 parts black
  1 part viridian green

Golden ochre

Venetian red

DOLLS' HOUSE

There is something comforting about an old fashioned handmade dolls' house and this one was inspired by a Victorian example. It makes the perfect way for children to pass the long winter evenings.

YOU WILL NEED

MATERIALS

sufficient ⅜-inch fiberboard to cut
  the following pieces:
    two 17 x 11 inches, for sides
    one 11½ x 19½ inches, for back
    one 19½ x 11 inches, for base
    two 10¼ x 8½ inches, for front
      panels
¼-inch fiberboard, cut as follows:
    one 21 x 8¾ inches, for front roof
    one 21 x 8½ inches, for back roof
¾-x-¾-inch softwood, two 12-inch
  lengths, for back corner
  reinforcements
⅜-x-1¼-inch softwood, two 12-inch
  lengths, for front corner
  reinforcements
¾-x-⅞-inch softwood, two 12-inch
  lengths, for front corner
  reinforcements
¾-x-1½-inch softwood, 17½-inch
  length, for top front strip
1¼-x-1¼-inch softwood, two 1½-inch
  lengths, for chimneys
1¾-inch softwood cube, cut in half
  diagonally, for dormer windows
2-inch triangular beading, two 2½-inch
  lengths, for dormer roofs
⅝-inch corner molding, 20-inch length,
  for roof ridge
¹⁄₁₆-x-½-inch softwood, 80-inch length,
  for door and window details
two pieces clear Plexiglas, 6 x
  5 inches, for windows
½-inch doweling, two ¾-inch lengths,
  for chimney pots
small door knob (with screw)

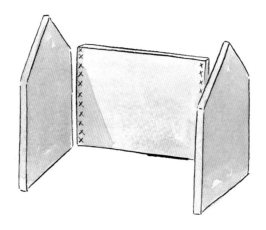

1 Cut out the back, sides, and front panels, using the template on page 89. Note that the top edge of the back panel is mitered to take the roof slope, making it 11½ inches on the outside edge and 12 inches on the inner edge. Join the sides to the back by gluing and butting the sides to the back. Clamp the joints while the glue sets and then insert finishing nails into the sides from the back.

2 Cut out the base and glue it in place inside the side and back panels. Hold the back corner reinforcements in position and mark the miter cut to match the roof line. Cut along these lines using a miter box and tenon saw, then glue the pieces in place.

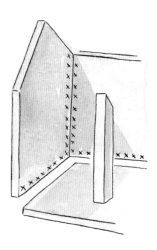

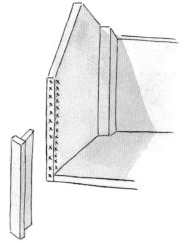

3 Glue the two parts of the front corner reinforcements together to make the shape shown, with the ⅜-x-⅞-inch inside pieces ⅜ inch shorter than the outside pieces so that they will sit on the base. Hold the assembled corner pieces in place and miter the top ends to match the roof line, as in step 2, then glue them in position.

4 Position the horizontal top front strip between the two side panels with its bottom edge 10¼ inches from the base. Mark the miter cut along it to match the roof line and cut away the wood with a plane or a file so that it will lie flush against the sloping roof, then glue the strip in place and insert a finishing nail through each end from the outside to provide additional strength.

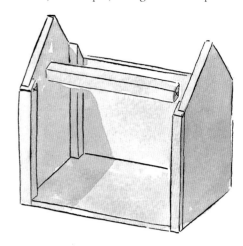

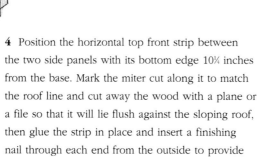

5 Mark the position of the windows on the two front panels in pencil, following the dotted lines on the template. Score along the lines with a craft knife, then drill a hole to take the saw blade. Cut out the windows using a saber saw or coping saw.

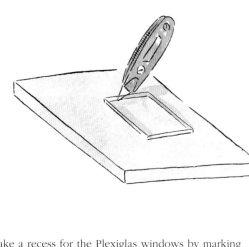

6 Make a recess for the Plexiglas windows by marking an ⅛-inch border around each window. Chisel this out to the depth of the Plexiglas.

7 Using a craft knife, cut the Plexiglas to fit in the recesses around each window. Then cut the ¹⁄₁₆-x-½-inch strip of wood into lengths to form the window frames. Lay the Plexiglas in place and glue the window-frame strips in position over it, butting the short strips up to the long ones.

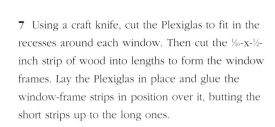

8 When these front panels are fixed in place, they will open to allow access to the inside of the dolls' house.

9 To make up the front door, cut the remainder of the ¹⁄₁₆-x-½-inch strip of wood into four lengths of 8 inches and eight lengths of ¾ inch. Assemble the door by gluing the strips onto the front panels at the inner edges as shown (see right), butting the short strips up to the longer lengths. Use a bradawl to make a pilot hole on the right-hand door for attaching the door knob, then screw it in place.

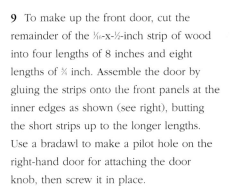

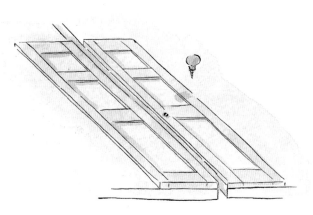

10 Mark the position for the hinges on the outside edges of the front panels and the front corner pieces. Score around them with a craft knife, then, using a chisel and mallet, create hinge mortises by hollowing out the wood to the depth of the hinges. Then screw the hinges in place.

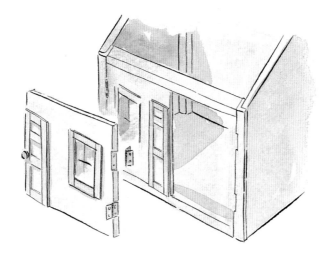

11 Make up the dormer windows by cutting two pieces of triangular beading to fit the 1¾-inch half-cube and the 45° angle of the dolls' house roof. Glue them together as shown, ensuring that the roofs overlap the half-cubes evenly on both sides. Then glue the dormer windows to the front roof piece.

12 Make up the roof by butting the back piece up to the front piece and gluing them together, then reinforce the joint with finishing nails. The angle of the butt joint is 90°.

    Attach the assembled roof to the base of the house, applying wood glue along all the adjoining edges. There should be an even overhang of ½ inch on all sides.

13 Drill a ½-inch hole in each chimney and insert a ¾-inch length dowel into each for the chimney pots. Cut a wedge out of the base of each chimney, so that it straddles the roof. Cut the corner molding into three lengths to fit along the top of the roof edge, allowing for the two chimneys to fit in between. Glue the molding and the chimneys to the ridge of the roof, butting them together.

14 Sand all the sharp edges and corners with medium, then fine, sandpaper to give them a rounded, friendly shape.

PAINT PALETTE AND EQUIPMENT

red oxide primer
artists' acrylic paints, in the following
  colors:
  white
  raw sienna
  cadmium yellow deep
  yellow ochre
  ultramarine
  raw umber
  red ochre
water
water-based satin varnish
antique oak wax polish
shallow white container, for mixing
broad household paintbrush
medium artists' brush
fine lining brush
2 pencil erasers
masking tape
2 strips of cardboard, 1¾ inch and
  2½ inch wide
rag
soft brush
soft cloth

PAINT SWATCHES

Orange-brown
3 parts white
2 parts raw sienna
2 parts cadmium yellow deep

Dark cream
I part yellow ochre
I part white

Cream
I part dark cream (as above)
I part white
I part water-based varnish

Slate
2 parts ultramarine
I part raw umber

Off-white
3 parts white
I part yellow ochre

Red ochre

STEPS TO PAINT

1 Using a broad household paintbrush, prime the whole dolls' house with an even coat of red oxide primer. Allow to dry overnight.

2 Mix about ½ cup of the orange-brown wall color—enough for two coats. Paint all the external walls and the front panels. Allow to dry, then apply a second coat.

3 Mix the dark cream paint and paint the window frames and the door, using the medium artists' brush. Then paint the inside walls using the broadest brush. Allow to dry before applying a second coat.

4 Mix up the slate roof color and paint the roof using the broadest brush. This color is opaque, so only one coat is needed. If wished, darken with a dash of red ochre and paint the ridge of the roof and the dormer roof sections, using the medium artists' brush. Allow to dry thoroughly overnight.

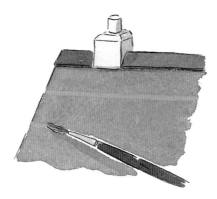

5 Make up a raised ruler the length of the roof by taping two pencil erasers to either end of a ruler. The idea is to raise the ruler above the surface so the metal part of the brush runs along the straight edge. The erasers provide a grip, so make sure you don't cover their base with the tape.

6 Paint the roof pattern in cream, thinning the paint with water so it flows easily. Using the narrowest strip of cardboard as a guide, mark the horizontal lines at 1¾-inch intervals, then paint them, front and back. Paint the vertical lines, aiming for 8 slates along the roof length.

7 Paint a brick effect on the walls of the house in the same way, using red ochre paint, thinned with water as necessary. The horizontal lines are 2½ inches apart; start at the base and work upwards, using the raised ruler as a guide and moving the erasers as you paint so that you always have a steady rest for the brush. When dry, add the vertical lines. Then paint the chimneys red ochre.

8 Divide the windows into panes using the off-white paint and a fine lining brush.

9 When the paint is dry, lightly sand the paintwork in places to simulate wear.

10 Use a rag to rub antique oak wax polish into the whole surface of the dolls' house. Apply the wax sparingly, starting on one side so that you see the effect and can gauge the amount of polish needed. Buff first with a soft brush, then with a soft cloth to achieve a high sheen.

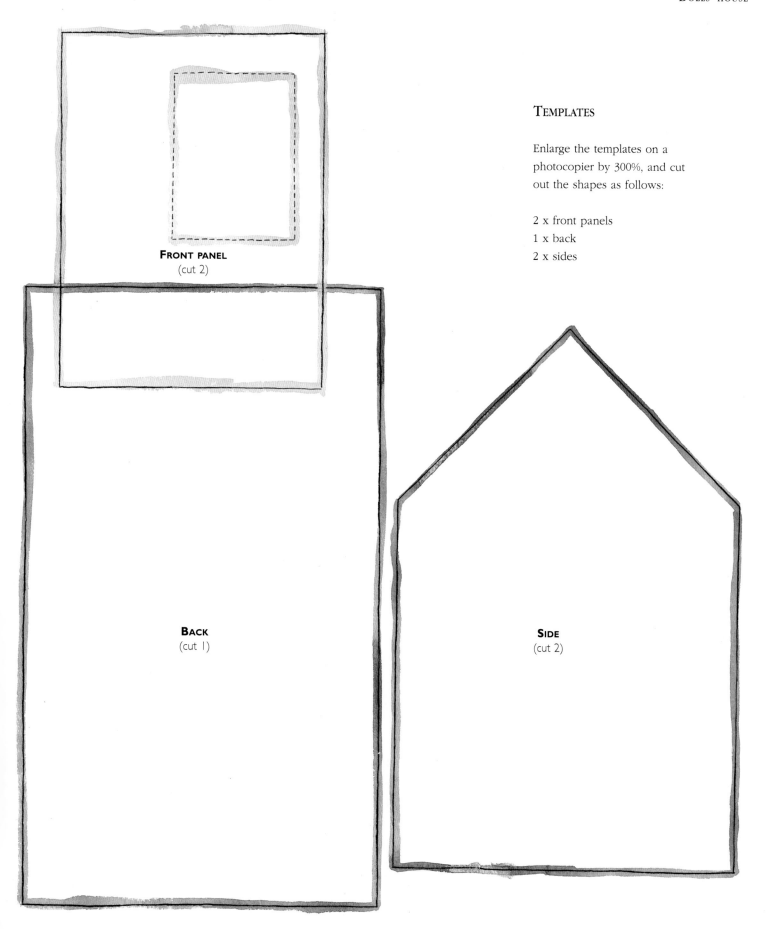

FRONT PANEL
(cut 2)

TEMPLATES

Enlarge the templates on a
photocopier by 300%, and cut
out the shapes as follows:

2 x front panels
1 x back
2 x sides

BACK
(cut 1)

SIDE
(cut 2)

Decorative Details

PICTURE FRAMES

Each of these three frames has been treated in a different way. They can stand alone, but also look very good as a group. Frames are not difficult to make, but accurate measuring, sawing, and mitering are vital.

DRIFTWOOD-EFFECT FRAME

1 For this frame, use framing softwood that already has a rabbet cut into it to hold the picture glass in place. Use a miter box and tenon saw to cut the softwood into two lengths of 12 inches and two of 8¼ inches, mitering the corners at 45°.

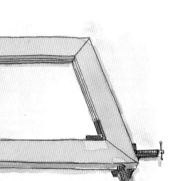

2 Glue the adjoining edges together to form a flat frame and clamp the corners with miter clamps until the glue has bonded. Then secure the mitered corner joints with corrugated fasteners before removing the clamps (see page 94, step 2).

3 Paint the frame following the directions in steps to paint (right).

4 Cut the hardboard to fit the back of the frame and have a glazier cut picture glass to fit inside. Secure the hardboard with metal framing clips, inserting them according to the manufacturer's instructions.

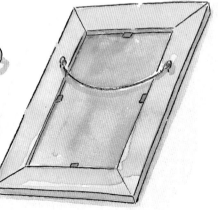

HANGING

Attach the ring and eye fittings one-third of the way down each side of the back of the frame. To hang the frame, thread picture wire through the ring fittings and secure the loose end by twisting it around the wire several times.

YOU WILL NEED

MATERIALS

¾-x-1¾-inch framing softwood with
    rabbet, 45-inch length
hardboard, approximately 8½ x
    4¾ inches, for backing (cut to fit)
picture glass, cut to fit

TOOLS AND EQUIPMENT

miter box
tenon saw
wood glue
miter clamps or framing clamps
4 corrugated fasteners
hammer
4 metal framing clips
2 ring and eye fittings
picture wire

PAINT PALETTE AND EQUIPMENT

white acrylic primer
burnt umber artists' oil paint
wax polish
broad artists' brush
medium and fine sandpaper
3 soft cloths

STEPS TO PAINT

1 Using a broad artists' brush, paint the frame with white acrylic primer and let dry.

2 Sand with medium and fine sandpaper, rounding off the edges slightly, so that some of the grain shows through.

3 Take a little burnt umber oil paint on a soft cloth and rub it into the surface, leaving subtle streaks of pure color in places. Allow to dry.

4 Apply a layer of clear wax polish, then rub off to a high sheen. Repeat until the right level of sheen is achieved.

YOU WILL NEED

MATERIALS

¾-x-2-inch softwood, 48-inch length

½-x-1-inch wooden beading, 84-inch
 length

hardboard, approximately 8 ×
 6 inches, for backing (cut to fit)

picture glass, cut to fit

TOOLS AND EQUIPMENT

miter box

tenon saw

wood glue

miter clamps or framing
 clamps

4 corrugated fasteners

hammer

ruler

4 metal framing clips

2 ring and eye fittings

picture wire

PAINT PALETTE AND EQUIPMENT

red ochre latex paint

gold size

Dutch metal leaf

crackle glazing varnish

viridian green artists' oil paint

turpentine

shellac

polyurethane satin varnish

broad artists' brush

steel wool

2 soft cloths

varnishing brush

fine sandpaper

RED AND GOLD FRAME

1 Use a miter box and tenon saw to cut two lengths of 12 inches, and two of 10 inches, mitering the corners at 45°.

2 Glue the four lengths of wood together to form a flat frame. Clamp the glued corners with miter clamps (see step 2, page 93), and reinforce the joints with corrugated fasteners before removing them.

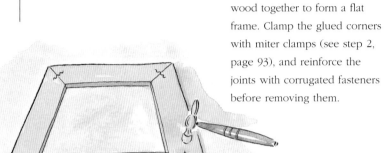

3 Using a miter box and tenon saw, cut the wooden beading into two lengths of 13 inches and two of 11 inches, mitering the corners to fit around the outside of the frame. Cut the remaining beading into two lengths of 8 inches and two of 6 inches to fit around the inside of the frame.

4 Glue the beading all around the outer edges, positioning it level with the back of the frame so that it extends forward to make a shallow box.

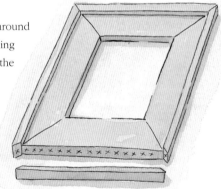

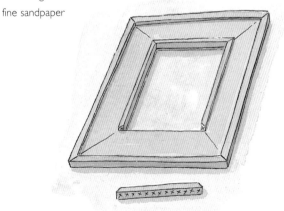

5 Glue the remaining beading around the inside edges, this time raising it ¼ inch from the back of the frame so that it protrudes ½ inch from the front of the frame. This raised inner rim will provide a rabbet to hold the glass in place.

Paint the frame following the directions in steps to paint (right).

6 Cut the hardboard to fit and have a glazier cut the picture glass. Secure with metal framing clips and attach picture wire for hanging (see page 93).

STEPS TO PAINT

1 Use a broad artists' brush to paint the frame with a base coat of red ochre latex paint.

2 When dry, apply gold size to the front and sides.

3 Press the sheets of Dutch metal leaf onto the tacky surface of the frame. Try to position the sheets so that fine cracks occur naturally where the red ochre shows through.

4 Once you have covered the entire frame, rub off any excess leaf with steel wool and polish with a soft cloth.

5 Follow the manufacturer's instructions to apply two coats of crackle glazing varnish. Allow to dry.

6 Pour a little viridian green artists' oil paint onto a soft cloth and rub well into the cracks, covering the whole frame.

7 Dampen the soft cloth slightly with turpentine, then rub off any viridian green from the surface. It will still be visible in the cracks.

8 Apply a coat of shellac. When dry, seal with several coats of varnish, rubbing the surface back with fine sandpaper between coats.

SQUARE, DEEP FRAME

1 Use a miter box and tenon saw to cut the narrower softwood into four equal 6-inch lengths, mitering the corners at 45°. Glue the pieces together at the corners to form the flat front of the frame. Clamp until the glue has dried and reinforce the joints with corrugated fasteners before removing the clamps (see page 94, step 2).

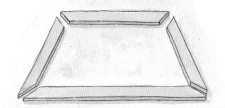

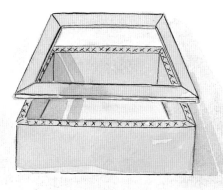

2 Using a miter box and tenon saw, cut the wider softwood into four equal 6-inch lengths, mitering the corners at 45°. These lengths fit together to form a deep box that is attached to the back of the flat frame.

3 Glue the four sides of the box together and clamp the corners until the glue has bonded. Then reinforce the joints with finishing nails for added strength.

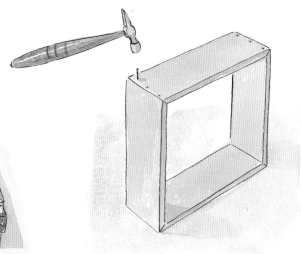

4 Glue the flat frame front onto the deep box and clamp until bonded.

5 Paint the frame following the directions in steps to paint (right).

6 Cut the hardboard to fit and have a glazier cut the picture glass. Secure with metal framing clips and attach picture wire to hang the frame (see page 93).

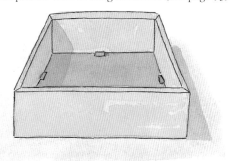

YOU WILL NEED

MATERIALS

½-x-1-inch softwood, 28-inch length, for front

½-x-4-inch softwood, 28-inch length, for sides

hardboard, approximately 5 x 5 inches, for backing (cut to fit)

picture glass, cut to fit

TOOLS AND EQUIPMENT

tenon saw

miter box

wood glue

4 miter clamps or framing clamps

4 corrugated fasteners

hammer

finishing nails

clamps

4 metal framing clips

2 ring and eye fittings

picture wire

PAINT PALETTE AND EQUIPMENT

red ochre latex paint

gilt cream

broad artists' brush

medium sandpaper

2 soft cloths

STEPS TO PAINT

1 Apply a base coat of red ochre latex paint to the front, inside edges, and sides of the box.

2 When dry, roughen the surface with medium sandpaper.

3 Apply the gilt cream to the roughened surface, rubbing it in well with a soft cloth so that some of the red shows through.

4 When dry, polish to give a shiny finish.

YOU WILL NEED

MATERIALS

⅛-inch grade A plywood (best
quality), 1 sheet

TOOLS AND EQUIPMENT

tracing paper
pencil
clamps
saber saw
medium and fine sandpaper
wood glue

PAINT PALETTE AND EQUIPMENT

white acrylic primer
artists' acrylic paints in the following
   colors:
   burnt sienna
   black
   raw sienna
   white
   yellow ochre
   ultramarine
   burnt umber
   cadmium red
   vermilion
   hooker's green
   cadmium yellow
   cobalt blue
   raw umber
   Venetian red
   oxide of chromium
   golden ochre
water
water-based satin varnish
shallow white container, for mixing
artists' brushes, Nos. 2, 4, and 6
small square-tipped varnishing brush

DECORATIONS

*Painted wooden decorations such as these are typical of European folk art,
and they can be scaled up or down to hang on the wall or to adorn a
Christmas tree. In time, they will become family heirlooms.*

4 Apply a coat of white acrylic primer to both sides of
the decorations and allow to dry. Sketch out the main
pattern divisions with a pencil, then paint the background
colors. When the paint is completely dry, add some of the
finer decorative details, using the templates as guides. To
make the shapes stand out, outline the bodies, wings,
antlers, feet, and tails with a medium shade, and allow to
dry. Finally, apply two coats of water-based satin varnish
according to the manufacturer's instructions.

1 Enlarge the animal templates on pages
98–9 on a photocopier, if required, then
transfer them onto the plywood, leaving sufficient room between each for cutting out.

2 Using clamps, secure the plywood to
a tabletop or workbench and cut out the
shapes with a saber saw.

3 Smooth any rough edges, first with
medium, then with fine, sandpaper.

5 To assemble the birds, position the
wings on the bodies, applying glue where
they overlap. Clamp the wings and bodies
together and leave to bond overnight.

PAINT SWATCHES

DEER RIGHT

Dark brown (outline)
2 parts burnt sienna
1 part black

Brown (horns)
(painted over yellow base coat)
1 part raw sienna
1 part water

Cream (head and legs)
2 parts white
1 part yellow ochre

Yellow (body and horns)
1 part raw sienna
1 part yellow ochre

Light blue (decorations)
3 parts ultramarine
3 parts white
1 part burnt umber

Dark blue (decorations)
3 parts ultramarine
1 part burnt umber
1 part white

White (decorations)

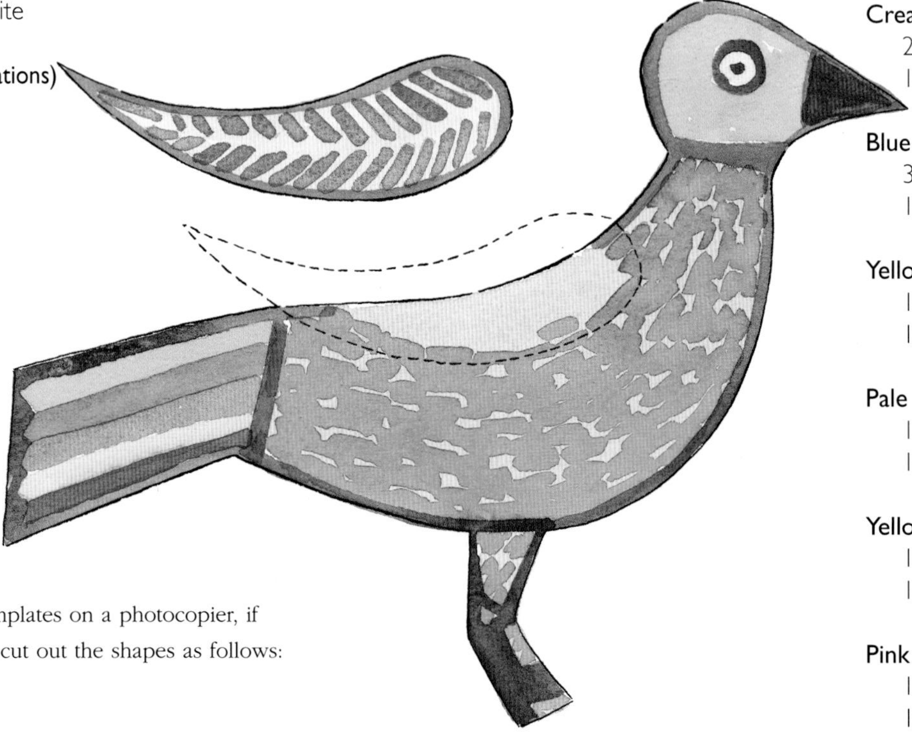

GREEN-HEADED BIRD BELOW

Dark brown (outline)
2 parts burnt sienna
1 part black

Red (beak and tail feather)
1 part cadmium red
1 part vermilion

Green (head and tail feather)
1 part hooker's green
1 part cadmium yellow

Cream (eye and wing)
2 parts white
1 part yellow ochre

Blue (wing stripes and tail feather)
3 parts cobalt blue
1 part raw umber

Yellow (body base colour)
1 part raw sienna
1 part yellow ochre

Pale orange (body and leg feathers)
1 part burnt sienna
1 part water

Yellow (tail feather)
1 part raw sienna
1 part yellow ochre

Pink (tail feather)
1 part cadmium red
1 part vermilion
1 part white

TEMPLATES

Enlarge the templates on a photocopier, if preferred, and cut out the shapes as follows:

1 x each body

2 x each set of wings

PARROT RIGHT

Brown (outline)
2 parts Venetian red
1 part raw sienna

Blue (head and feet)
3 parts cobalt blue
1 part raw umber
1 part white

Orange (eye and body)
2 parts raw sienna
1 part yellow ochre

Cream (beak and decorations)
2 parts white
1 part yellow ochre

Blue (head and feet details)
3 parts cobalt blue
1 part raw umber

Red (breast)
1 part Venetian red
1 part cadmium red

Dark blue (neck and tail)
3 parts cobalt blue
1 part raw umber

Terra-cotta (neck, wing and tail)
2 parts Venetian red
2 parts raw sienna
1 part white

Beige (wing top)
2 parts white
1 part yellow ochre
1 part raw sienna

Blue (wings)
4 parts cobalt blue
1 part raw umber
1 part white

Green (wings)
1 part oxide of chromium
1 part water

Yellow (wings)
1 part yellow ochre
1 part water

PIGEON ABOVE

Dark brown (outlines and breast decorations)
2 parts burnt sienna
1 part black

Red-brown (tail and wing)
2 parts Venetian red
1 part raw sienna

Ochre (head, wing, and feet)
1 part raw sienna
1 part golden ochre

Gray (tail and wing)
2 parts cobalt blue
1 part raw umber

Gray-blue (breast)
3 parts cobalt blue
2 parts white
1 part raw umber

Blue (neck rings)
2 parts cobalt blue
1 part white

White (details)

WINDOW BOX

This rustic window box looks as if it belongs on a painted horse-drawn gypsy caravan. There are no fancy joints—making it easy to put together using a hammer and nails. The scalloped shapes can be cut out with a saber saw or coping saw.

YOU WILL NEED

MATERIALS

sufficient ¾-inch reclaimed wood,
    such as floorboards, or softwood
    to cut the following pieces:
    one 8 × 24½ inches, for back
    two 8 × 8 inches, for sides
    one approximately 24 × 7¼ inches,
    for base (cut to fit)
¾-x-½-inch softwood, 80-inch length,
    for horizontal rails and vertical
    struts

TOOLS AND EQUIPMENT

tracing paper
pencil
saber saw or coping saw
clamps
medium and fine sandpaper
wood glue
finishing nails
hammer
strip of cardboard, 2 inches wide

1 Using a photocopier, enlarge the templates on pages 104–5 by 160%. Trace the pattern shapes and transfer them onto the wood.

2 Clamp the wood to the edge of a workbench or tabletop and cut out the back and sides with a saber saw or coping saw. Smooth down the scalloped edges with sandpaper to remove any rough fibers.

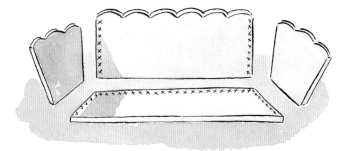

3 The sides butt up to the back. Glue the adjoining edges and reinforce with finishing nails, tapping them through from the back. Mark the dimensions for the base and cut it out. Glue the assembled sides onto the base, flush with the edges, then strengthen with finishing nails.

4 Cut the ¾-x-½-inch softwood into two 23-inch lengths to form the horizontal rails. Cut the remainder into ten 3¼-inch lengths to form the vertical struts. Glue and nail the bottom rail along the front edge.

5 Fix one vertical strut at each end, on top of the bottom rail and against the sides of the window box. Glue and nail. Rest the top rail on top of the vertical end struts. Then glue and nail it in place.

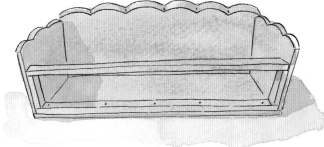

6 Using your strip of cardboard to guide you, position the remaining vertical struts at equal 2-inch intervals along the bottom rail. Apply a little glue to the end of each strut and slide them in between the horizontal rails. For extra strength, reinforce with finishing nails, tapping them through the top rail and into the vertical struts.

PAINT PALETTE AND EQUIPMENT

artists' acrylic or oil paints in the following colors:
  hooker's green
  cobalt blue
  white
  cadmium yellow
  Venetian red
  burnt umber
  ultramarine
  raw umber
  yellow ochre
matte varnish (water-based with
  acrylics for indoor use, or poly-
    urethane with oils for outdoor use)
shallow white container, for mixing
broad and small household paintbrushes
No. 5 artists' and No. 3 lining brushes

STEPS TO PAINT

1 With a broad household paintbrush, paint the base, sides, and back of the box, using the green background color (see paint swatches, opposite). When dry, use a smaller brush to paint the horizontal rails and scalloped top edges blue. Then, paint the vertical struts red.

2 Mark out eight evenly spaced circles, 1½ inches in diameter, along the back and sides to form the flower centers. Paint the flowers in your choice of colors (see below and opposite).

3 Leave to dry overnight, then seal the entire box with two coats of varnish.

FLOWER A

1 Using a No. 5 artists' brush, paint the center of each flower pinkish red, dark blue or brown (see paint swatches, opposite). Allow to dry.

2 Paint four leaves around the flower center using hooker's green and a clean No. 5 artists' brush. Allow to dry.

3 Using a No. 3 lining brush, add the center details and daisy-shaped petals in pink, cream or yellow. Allow to dry.

4 Paint a small yellow-cream stamen in the center and surround it with a circle of dots.

5 Add the yellow veins on the leaves with a clean No. 3 lining brush.

6 Finish with decorative flourishes around each flower in hooker's green.

102

PAINT SWATCHES

Green (background)
3 parts hooker's green
I part cobalt blue
I part white
I part cadmium yellow

Red (vertical railings)
3 parts Venetian red
I part white

Blue (horizontal railings)
3 parts cobalt blue
I part burnt umber
I part white

CENTERS (VARIOUS)

Pinkish red
2 parts white
I part Venetian red

Dark blue
3 parts ultramarine
I part raw umber

Brown
2 parts yellow ochre
I part burnt umber

Green (leaves)
hooker's green

PETALS AND LEAF VEINS (VARIOUS)

Pink
2 parts Venetian red
2 parts white

Cream
3 parts white
I part raw umber

Yellow
3 parts yellow ochre
I part white

Cream-yellow (stamens)
2 parts white
I part yellow ochre

FLOWER B

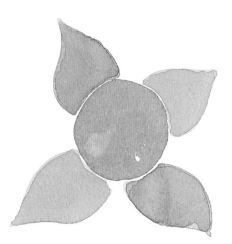

1 Using a No. 5 brush, paint the flower centers pinkish red, dark blue or brown (see paint swatches, above). Allow to dry.

2 Add four green leaves around the center in hooker's green. Allow to dry.

3 Paint the rose-shaped petals individually, in pink, cream, or yellow. Allow to dry.

4 Add the delicate cream-yellow flower stamens with a clean No. 3 lining brush.

5 Use the fine No. 3 lining brush to add the yellow veins to the leaves.

6 Finish with several flourishes around the outside in hooker's green.

103

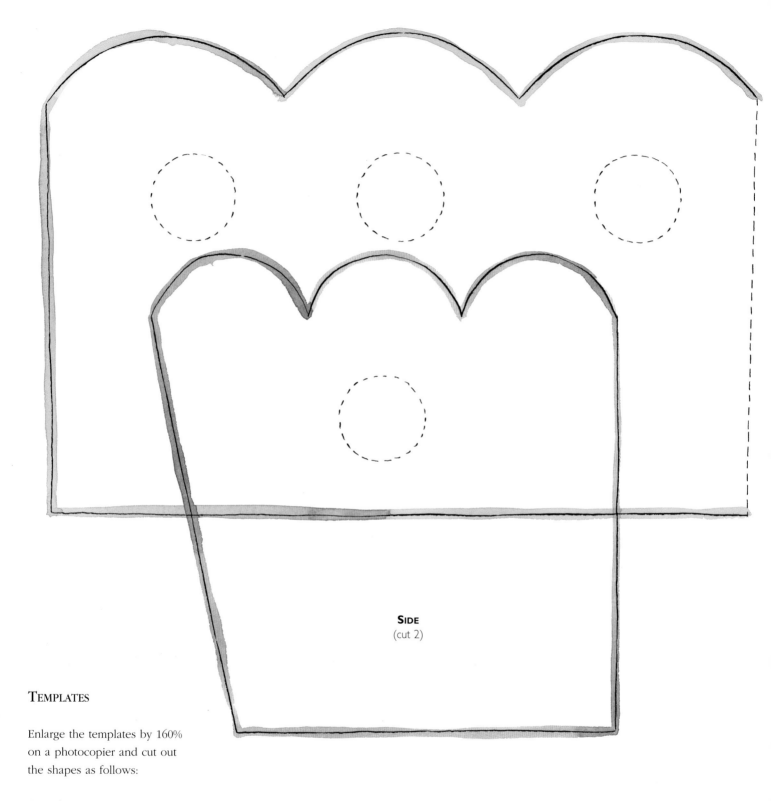

SIDE
(cut 2)

TEMPLATES

Enlarge the templates by 160%
on a photocopier and cut out
the shapes as follows:

2 x sides
1 x back

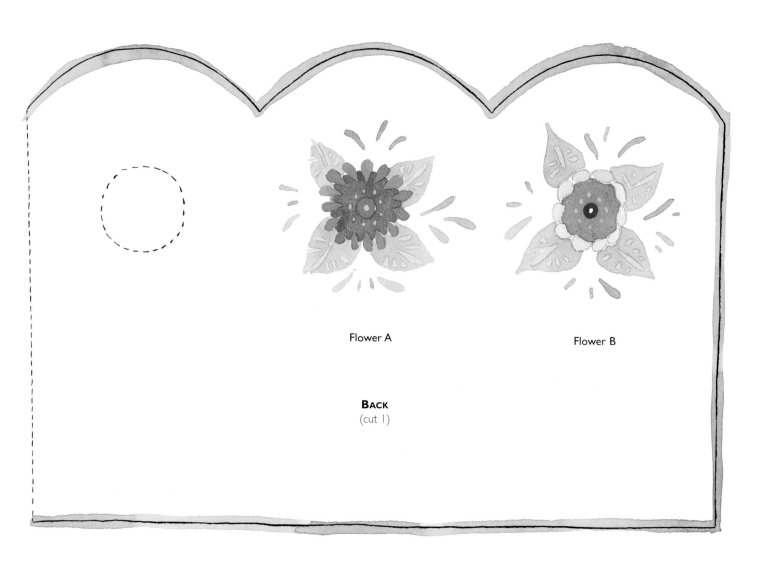

Flower A

Flower B

BACK
(cut 1)

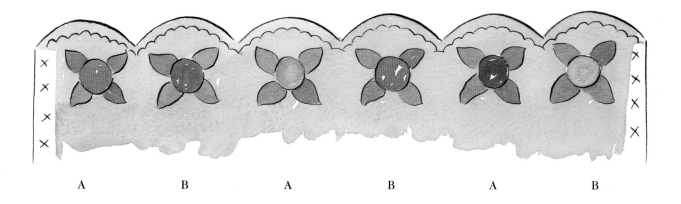

A B A B A B

Paint the two flower shapes alternately, in any combination of colors you
wish (see pages 102–3). Apply blue paint to the scalloped top edges.

DOOR KNOBS AND LIGHT PULLS

Small details like these can add a stylish, personal touch to a room. Three styles are shown here, all of which can be adapted using different color combinations. You may wish to continue the theme elsewhere in the room—on a lamp shade, for example.

YOU WILL NEED

MATERIALS, TOOLS, AND EQUIPMENT

sufficient 1¼-x-1¼-inch softwood to cut
  one 5-inch length for each light pull

standard wooden door knobs

tenon saw

vise

hand drill, with ¼-inch and ½-inch
  twist bits

medium half-round file

medium and fine sandpaper

PAINT PALETTE AND EQUIPMENT

artists' acrylic paints in the following
  colors:
  cream
  Venetian red
  ultramarine
  burnt umber
  hooker's green

water-based satin varnish

shallow white container, for mixing

small household paintbrush

small natural sponge

No. 5 long-bristled lining brush

fine artists' brush

No. 2 lining brush

strip of cardboard, about ¼ inch wide

1 To make the light pulls, first cut the wood into 5-inch lengths with a tenon saw.

2 Hold it firmly in the vise and use a ¼-inch bit to drill a hole all the way through its length for the cord.

3 Use a ½-inch bit to make the hole slightly larger at one end to take the knotted cord.

4 File and sand the four edges of the opposite end to the same angle to give a beveled top (see right). Alternatively, use medium and fine sandpaper to smooth the four corners to give a more rounded shape, leaving the top flat.

STEPS TO PAINT

1 Use a small household paintbrush to paint the knobs and light pulls cream. To prevent smudging as you paint, hold a pencil inserted into one end of the light pull.

2 For the spongeware effect, dip the natural sponge into the red paint and press lightly on all sides.

3 For the gingham light pull, make a cardboard marker the width of a brushstroke (about ¼ inch wide). Beginning at the beveled end, paint three long blue stripes on each side. Allow to dry before painting the intersecting stripes, one side at a time. For the door knob, begin with a central stripe, then paint stripes on each side. Allow to dry, then add the intersecting stripes. Make up a darker blue by using less varnish, then add a dark stripe down the middle of each stripe with the No. 2 lining brush. Paint the lowest ridge of the knob in blue.

4 For the fern light pull, paint a long green wavy line down the middle of each side. Then add the fronds. Finish with a flower shape at the beveled end and a stripe around the top and bottom. For the door knob, paint a circle in the center and surround with fronds. Finish with a green border around the lowest ridge.

5 When dry, seal with two coats of satin varnish.

PAINT SWATCHES

Cream (background)

Red (spongeware)
  3 parts Venetian red
  1 part water-based varnish

Blue (gingham)
  2 parts ultramarine
  1 part burnt umber
  1 part water-based varnish

Green (fern)
  3 parts hooker's green
  few drops Venetian red
  1 part water-based varnish

Door Numbers

These house numbers are a great way of stamping your identity on your home. There are ten variations here, each using a single house number on a small wooden shape.

YOU WILL NEED

MATERIALS, TOOLS, AND EQUIPMENT

any scrap wood

tracing paper

pencil

cramps

saber saw or coping saw

medium and fine sandpaper

drill, with ³⁄₃₂-inch screw bit

small wood screws

PAINT PALETTE AND EQUIPMENT

For all door numbers:

artists' acrylic paints in the following
   colors (see individual swatches):
   white
   cobalt blue
   burnt umber
   ultramarine
   cream
   cadmium red deep
   cadmium yellow
   black
   vermilion
   Indian red
   navy blue
   Venetian red
   hooker's green
   cadmium yellow deep
   yellow ochre

water-based satin varnish

shallow white container, for mixing

small household paintbrush

selection of artists' and lining brushes

stencil brush

1 On a photocopier, enlarge your chosen shape from pages 110–11 to your required size and transfer it onto the wood. Clamp, and cut out the shape with a saber saw or coping saw.

2 Sand the edges to round them off, then drill two small holes to carry the screws.

PAINT SWATCHES

No.1

White (background)

Blue (number and border)
   1 part cobalt blue
   1 part burnt umber

No. 2

Gray (background)
   3 parts white
   2 parts ultramarine
   1 part burnt umber

White (number)

No. 3

Cream (background)

Red (number)
   cadmium red deep

Dark green (inner border)
   2 parts ultramarine
   1 part cadmium yellow

Light green (outer border)
   4 parts white
   1 part green (as above)

No. 4

Cream (background)
   white (sealed with
      shellac)

Blue (top coat)
   5 parts ultramarine
   1 part burnt umber

No. 5

Cream (background)

Pink (border)
   4 parts white
   1 part cadmium red deep

Black (number and lines)

No. 6

Reddish brown (background)
   2 parts vermilion
   1 part Indian red
   1 part burnt umber

Cream (number)
   white (sealed with
      shellac)

No. 7

Dark blue (background)
   navy blue

No. 8

Cream (background)

Brown (number)
   1 part burnt umber
   1 part Venetian red

Red (border)
   2 parts water-based
      varnish
   1 part Venetian red

No. 9

Cream (background)

Green (number and borders)
   hooker's green

No. 10

Cream (background)

Yellow (top coat)
   2 parts cadmium yellow
      deep
   2 parts white
   1 part yellow ochre

Reddish brown (number)
   2 parts burnt umber
   1 part Venetian red

ADDITIONAL MATERIALS

No. 1
crackle glazing varnish
raw umber artists' acrylic paint
soft cloth

No. 2
antiquing varnish

No. 3
stencil cardboard or sheet of clear
  plastic
spray adhesive
craft knife

No. 4
paper
craft knife
spray adhesive
natural sponge
shellac

No. 5
card for template
craft knife
spray adhesive
antiquing glaze

No. 6
water
textured fabric, such as canvas
shellac

No. 7
gold size
Dutch metal leaf
fine steel wool

No. 8
stencil cardboard or sheet of clear
  plastic
spray adhesive
craft knife

No. 9
antiquing glaze

No. 10
stencil cardboard or sheet of clear
  plastic
spray adhesive

NUMBER ONE

Paint the background white and let dry. Trace the number and border, transfer them onto the wood and paint them in blue. When dry, sand lightly, then apply crackle glazing varnish, according to the manufacturer's instructions. Rub a little raw umber into the cracks, then rub off with a soft cloth. When dry, seal with two coats of water-based satin varnish, allowing it to dry between coats.

NUMBER TWO

Mix up the colors for the gray background and apply to the wood. When dry, sand back lightly, then trace the number, transfer it onto the wood and paint it white. Let dry. Apply the antiquing varnish and allow to dry. Then seal with two coats of water-based satin varnish, allowing for drying times between coats.

NUMBER SIX

Paint the wood reddish brown. Make a glaze using one part background color, one part burnt umber, and two parts varnish; thin with water as necessary. Paint on, then press a piece of textured fabric onto the wet glaze. Peel off, allow to dry, then paint the number in white. Apply a coat of shellac, which will yellow the white paint, then varnish.

NUMBER SEVEN

Paint the background dark blue. Trace the number and border and transfer them onto the wood. Apply gold size to the outlined areas, then cover the tacky area with Dutch metal leaf. Burnish with fine steel wool and apply two coats of varnish, allowing it to dry between coats.

NUMBER THREE

Paint the wood cream and let dry. Trace the number 3, spray the back of the tracing with adhesive and stick it onto stencil cardboard or clear plastic. Cut out with a craft knife and trim the card to fit the inner panel, clipping the corners. Stick the stencil in place and paint the number in red with a stencil brush, then paint around the edge of the cardboard in dark green. Add four parts white and paint the pale green outer edge. Varnish when dry.

NUMBER FOUR

Paint the wood with white paint. Draw the number 4 on paper and cut it out. Use spray adhesive to stick it down in the center of the wood. Mix up the blue paint and apply it with a natural sponge over and around the paper. Let dry. Peel off the paper mask to reveal a white number 4. Apply a coat of shellac, which will yellow the white paint. When dry, apply two coats of varnish, allowing for drying times between coats.

NUMBER FIVE

Paint the wood cream. Cut out a piece of cardboard to act as a template for the inner square. Cut off one corner and use spray adhesive to stick it down in the center of the panel. Paint the border pink, leave to dry, then peel off the template. With a fine lining brush, paint a black border around the outer edge and a second border around the central panel, then paint the number 5. Varnish, then apply antiquing glaze, then varnish again, allowing for drying times between coats.

NUMBER EIGHT

Paint the wood cream and let dry. Paint the border red, using pressed brushstrokes to make the pattern. Trace the number 8, stick it onto stencil cardboard or clear plastic and cut it out with a craft knife. Stick the stencil in place and paint the number 8 in brown with a stencil brush. Let dry, then varnish.

NUMBER NINE

Paint the background with cream paint and allow to dry. Trace the number 9 and the borders and transfer them onto the wood. Use a fine lining brush to paint the green areas and allow to dry. Varnish, then apply the antiquing glaze, followed by another coat of varnish.

NUMBER TEN

Paint the wood with cream base coat. Then, using a very dry brush, paint a thin coat of yellow over the top. Stencil the number 10 (as for numbers 3 and 8), in reddish brown, allowing paint to build up around the stencil and creep under the edges slightly, giving a blurred effect. Sand lightly and varnish twice.

LAMP BASE

This urn-shaped lamp base is created from four identical shapes of wood that are glued together. A channel is chiseled down the center to take the wiring, then the four pieces are joined together.

YOU WILL NEED

MATERIALS

sufficient 1-inch softwood to cut
   the following pieces:
   four 11¾ x 8⅛ inches
screw-on lamp fitting, with
   extension tube to give height
   (4¾ inches used here)
cord and plug
piece of felt, approximately
   4 x 8⅛ inches, for base (cut to fit)

TOOLS AND EQUIPMENT

tracing paper
pencil
clamps
saber saw
try square
chisel
mallet
wood glue
medium and fine sandpaper

PAINT PALETTE AND EQUIPMENT

artists' acrylic paints in the following
   colors:
   black
   cadmium orange
   golden ochre
fine felt-tipped pen
   (water-based ink)
medium felt-tipped pen
   (water-based ink)
alcohol-based aerosol varnish
polyurethane satin varnish
shallow white container, for mixing
broad household paintbrush
varnishing brush

1 Using a photocopier, enlarge the template on page 115 by 130%. Then trace the shape of the lamp base and transfer it onto the four pieces of softwood.

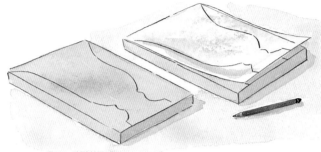

2 Using clamps, secure each piece of wood individually onto a tabletop or workbench, then cut out the identical shapes using a saber saw.

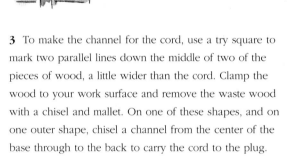

3 To make the channel for the cord, use a try square to mark two parallel lines down the middle of two of the pieces of wood, a little wider than the cord. Clamp the wood to your work surface and remove the waste wood with a chisel and mallet. On one of these shapes, and on one outer shape, chisel a channel from the center of the base through to the back to carry the cord to the plug.

4 To assemble the base, apply wood glue along the inner surfaces of both center pieces, taking care that the glue doesn't seep into the channels. Then glue on the two outer shapes in the same way. Clamp the four shapes together and leave overnight until the glue has bonded.

5 When the glue is dry, use medium, then fine, sandpaper to smooth the edges of the lamp base so that the joins don't show.

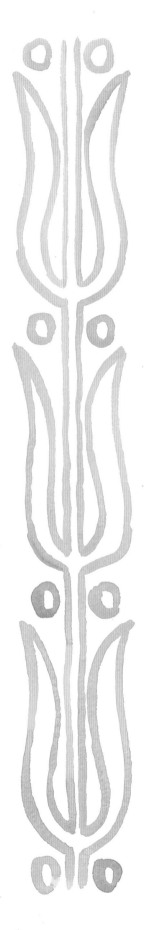

PAINT SWATCHES

Black

Orange

    I part cadmium orange
    I part golden ochre

STEPS TO PAINT

1 Using a broad household paintbrush and black paint, start by painting the back, top, and sides of the lamp base. If necessary, apply two coats of paint to achieve a good, even coverage, allowing it to dry between coats.

2 Next, apply two coats of orange paint to the front of the lamp base. Take extra care around the edges. Allow to dry.

3 Place a sheet of tracing paper over your enlarged photocopy and carefully trace the patterns. Turn your tracing over and go over the outlines with a soft pencil.

4 Place your tracing right-side-up on the front of the lamp base and transfer the pattern onto the painted wood.

5 The black detailing is added in felt-tipped pen. Use a fine pen to go over the pencil outlines, then fill in the patterns with a medium-tipped pen, taking care not to smudge the ink.

6 Once you are happy with the design, seal the ink with an alcohol-based aerosol varnish. (Do not use a water-based varnish or the pattern will run.) Allow to dry for one hour.

7 Apply two coats of polyurethane satin varnish to the whole lamp base, allowing the varnish to dry completely between coats.

STEPS TO ASSEMBLE

1 Take the lamp base to an electrician to insert the fitting. If you are using the long stem-type fitting (see below), you may need to drill a wider hole down the middle of the lamp base, from the top, to take the pipe.

2 To finish, glue a piece of felt, cut to size, onto the bottom of the lamp base. This will hold the cord in place and prevent the base from scratching your tabletop.

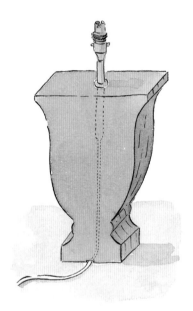

1

2

LAMP BASE
(cut 4)

TEMPLATE

Enlarge the template by 130% on a photocopier and cut out the shapes as follows:

4 x lamp bases

MODEL BOAT

Model boats like this were made before the days of mass-production, and an original is worth a small fortune on the antique market. This one does not pretend to be anything but a copy, but it is still a lot of fun to age a new wooden piece artificially.

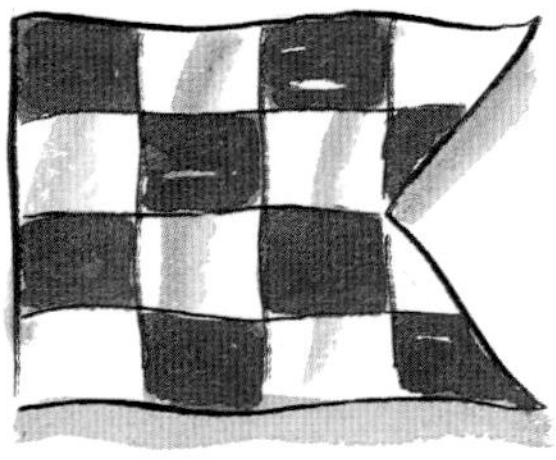

YOU WILL NEED

MATERIALS

- sufficient 1-inch softwood to cut the following shapes:
  - five 23⅜ x 5 inches, for hull
- ⅜-inch wooden doweling, 38-inch length, for masts
- ¼-inch wooden doweling, 6-inch length, for spur
- ⅛-inch plywood, cut as follows:
  - two 1¼ x 5¼ inches, for wheelhouse sides
  - two 1¼ x 3¼ inches, for wheelhouse ends
- ¼-inch plywood, 5½ x 3½ inches, for wheelhouse roof
- ¼-x-¼-inch softwood, 17-inch length, for railings
- $\frac{3}{32}$-inch wooden doweling, 18-inch length (or 24 matchsticks), for struts
- ½-x-1¾-inch softwood, 3-inch length, for steps
- 1 cork, ¾-inch diameter, cut into 2
- ¾-inch steel piping, two 2¼-inch lengths, for funnels
- ¼-inch softwood, four ⅝ x 2 inches, for rigging struts
- 4 round-headed wood screws
- ball of string, for rigging
- two miniature flags

TOOLS AND EQUIPMENT

- tracing paper and pencil
- ruler
- clamps
- saber saw and tenon saw
- hand drill with ½-inch, ⅜-inch, ¼-inch and $\frac{3}{32}$-inch twist bits
- wood glue
- plane
- medium and fine sandpaper
- craft knife
- finishing nails and hammer
- screwdriver

1 Using a photocopier, enlarge the template on page 119. Trace the shape of the boat base and transfer it onto the five lengths of wood. On the fifth one, mark a ⅜-inch border around the inside of the shape.

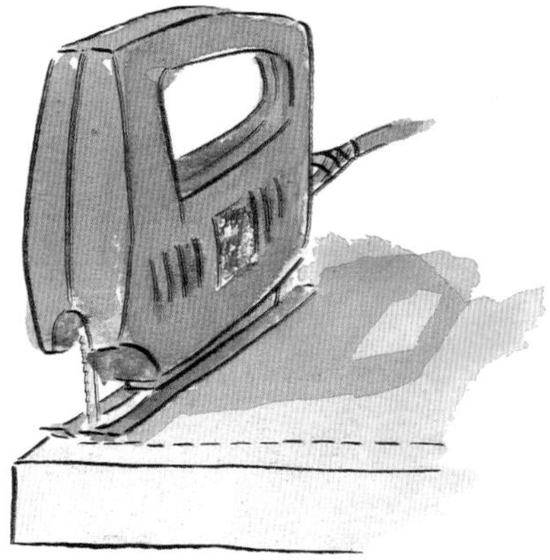

2 Clamp the wood to a steady surface and use a saber saw to cut out all five shapes exactly the same. Each piece must be cut individually to ensure accuracy. In the fifth one, drill a hole for the saw blade on the inside of and close to the marked line, then cut out and discard the middle of the boat shape, leaving the ⅜-inch border intact, which will form the deck edge.

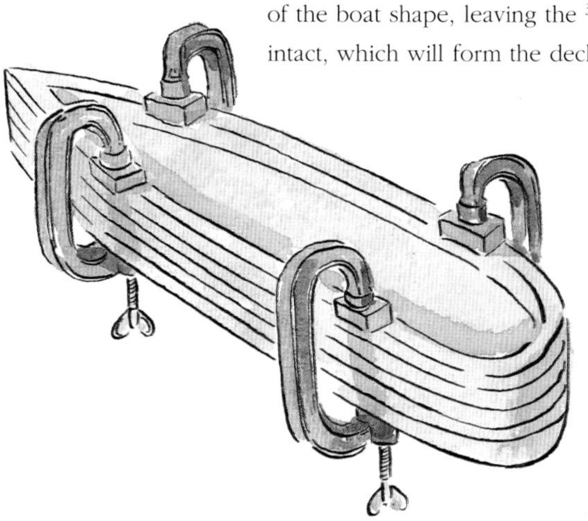

3 To make up the height of the hull, stack up the four intact boat shapes in layers. Make sure all edges line up exactly before applying wood glue to all adjoining surfaces. Finally, glue the cut-out deck edge on top. Fit clamps evenly all around the edges as shown and leave until bonded.

4 Plane the deck edge so it slopes from the bow and levels off to the stern. The bow should be ⅛–¼ inch higher than the stern. Sand the sides of the hull, so the boat looks as if it has been cut from a single piece of wood.

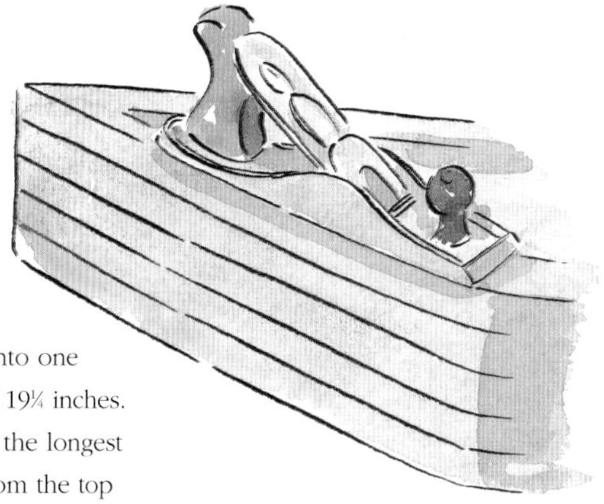

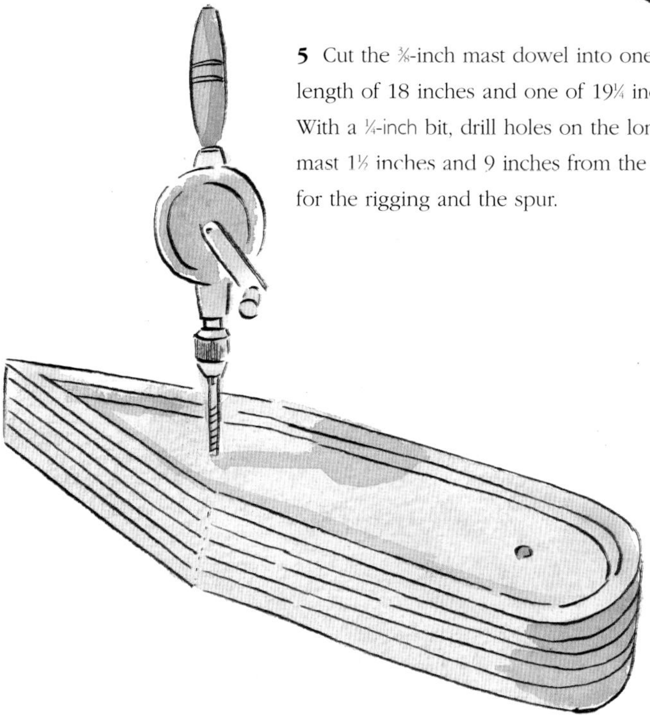

5 Cut the ⅜-inch mast dowel into one length of 18 inches and one of 19¼ inches. With a ¼-inch bit, drill holes on the longest mast 1½ inches and 9 inches from the top for the rigging and the spur.

6 For the upper and lower rigging, drill holes on the shortest mast 1¼ inches and 8 inches from the top. Using a ⅜-inch bit, drill holes in the deck 1⅝ inches deep for the masts; drill the hole at the stern at 70° to take the rear sloping mast and the hole at the bow at 90° for the upright mast. Shave the bottom of both masts so they fit snugly into the holes, then fix with wood glue. Place a spot of glue on the end of the spur and fix it on the sloping mast.

7 To make the wheelhouse that sits on the deck, first drill the portholes along the two long sides of the plywood. Make four ½-inch diameter holes on each side, spacing them ½ inch from each end with ¾ inch between them. Make up the wheelhouse as shown, butting up the sides to the shorter ends and gluing them together. Clamp and allow to bond.

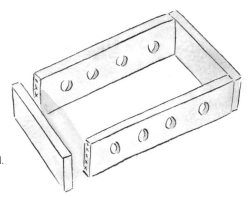

8 Cut the railing to fit around the edge of the wheelhouse roof, leaving a gap at one end (see template). Glue the railing together at the four corners. When dry, clamp the railing on top of the wheelhouse roof and, using a ³⁄₃₂-inch bit, drill 24 small holes at evenly spaced intervals through the railing and into the wheelhouse roof.

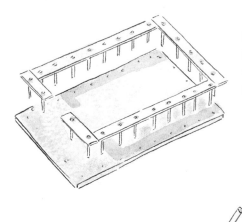

9 Cut the ³⁄₃₂-inch dowel for the struts into 24 lengths, each ¾ inch. Glue the dowels, or matchsticks, into the drilled holes in the railings and the wheelhouse roof. Sand the railings to level off any protruding ends. Glue the roof onto the wheelhouse.

10 Cut the wood for the steps into three lengths, of 1½ inches, 1 inch, and ½ inch. Glue them together to form a stack (see above).

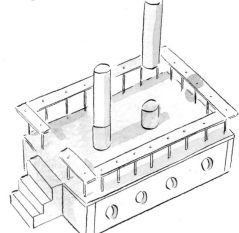

11 Glue the half-corks to the top of the wheelhouse and attach the piping for the funnels snugly on top. Glue the steps to the front end of the wheelhouse and then glue the whole thing in position on the deck, using the template on page 119 as a guide.

12 Using a ³⁄₃₂-inch bit, drill three holes in each of the rigging struts and glue, then nail them in position on the side of the boat (see template). Insert three rigging screws at the stern and one at the bow, as shown on the template.

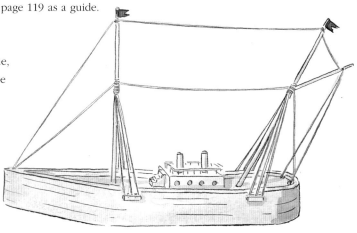

13 Paint and varnish the boat, then allow to dry. Cut lengths of string and knot them below the holes in the struts, taking them up to the mast, where they are tied and glued. Knot a length of string to the rigging screws and attach to the masts (see right). There is just a small amount of whipping on each mast to cover the joining pieces. Finally, add the flags.

PAINT PALETTE AND EQUIPMENT

white acrylic primer
artists' acrylic paints, as in paint swatches,
 below
water-based satin varnish
dark oak antiquing varnish
shallow white container, for mixing
selection of artists' brushes
No. 3 lining brush
varnishing brush
soft cloth

PAINT SWATCHES

Cadmium scarlet

Sap green

Lemon yellow

Ultramarine

Golden ochre

Venetian red

Raw umber

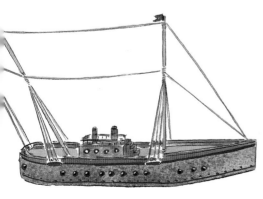

STEPS TO PAINT

1 Paint the whole boat with white acrylic primer and let dry.

2 Mix one part lemon yellow to five parts ultramarine and use to paint the hull, stopping about ¾ inch from the top edge at the stern and 1¼ inches from the top edge at the bow (because of the slope). Let dry.

3 Mix one part ultramarine to eight parts Venetian red and use to paint the ¾–1¼-inch strip around the top of the hull. Don't forget the inside of the deck edge. Reserve some of this colored paint for step 5. Let dry.

4 Mix one part Venetian red to six parts golden ochre and use to paint the deck and wheelhouse. Let dry.

5 Using the remaining color from step 3, paint eleven portholes on each side of the hull and three on the stern. Also paint the masts, steps, the edge of the wheelhouse roof, the anchor and the railings. Let dry.

6 Using cadmium scarlet, paint a ⅛-inch border around the portholes on the sides of the hull and on the wheelhouse. Paint the funnels, rigging struts, base of the mast and rigging screws the same color. Using a fine lining brush, paint a red plimsoll line ⅝ inch from the bottom of the hull with a dotted line ⅛ inch above it, and a similar line under the top strip painted in step 3. Paint red crosses on both ends of the steps. Paint three stripes on the funnels with sap green. Let dry.

7 Mix one part raw umber to five parts white primer and use to highlight the portholes and to paint the name.

8 When completely dry, apply the dark oak antiquing varnish, wiping it off before it dries so that it clings in the corners and just yellows the paint colors. Let dry.

9 Seal the boat with two coats of water-based satin varnish.

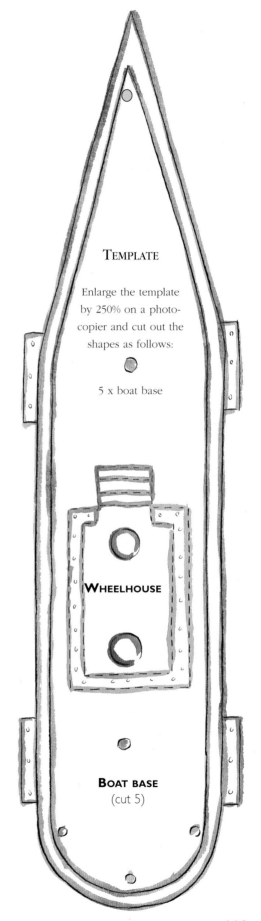

TEMPLATE

Enlarge the template by 250% on a photocopier and cut out the shapes as follows:

5 x boat base

WHEELHOUSE

BOAT BASE
(cut 5)

119

Wood Guide

The main classifications for types of wood are softwood, hardwood, and manufactured board. All the projects featured in this book are designed to be made from either softwood or manufactured board, rather than hardwood, which is more expensive to buy and less easy to work with.

Bear in mind that as good-quality softwood can also be expensive, you do not necessarily have to buy new wood. Old wood, like floorboards, has a wonderful textured appearance that can often be exploited in the course of your decoration to create a distressed, aged look.

Softwood

The term softwood refers to botanical grouping of the wood, rather than its physical properties. It is the open-grained wood of any coniferous tree, such as spruce, fir, and pine. When softwood is converted into boards, it can be identified by its relatively light range of colors, from pale yellow to reddish brown.

Most softwood is strong in the direction of the grain, but weak across it. Its main advantage over hardwood, other than its less expensive price, is that it is very lightweight and easy to saw, chisel, plane, and sand. It holds screws well, but nails can cause splitting, especially if they are used in a line along the grain.

When making objects for outdoor use, bear in mind that softwood is a porous material and must be treated with a preservative or coated with varnish to make it weatherproof.

Although lumberyards sell softwood in standard sizes, which are either PAR (planed all round), or sawn size, true measurements can often vary from nominal measurements by up to ⅛ inch on all sides.

In addition, softwood used by the building trade is not suitable for these projects as it is not seasoned (dried out) properly and therefore has a tendency to warp in the warm environment of the home.

Softwoods are graded according to the evenness of the grain and the amount of allowable defects such as knots. It is also stress-graded for structural use where strength is important. When buying wood, remember that it is an organic material and no two pieces will ever be the same. Check it carefully before buying and discard any that is faulty. The main defects to look out for are:

- knots, which make sawing impossible and also ooze resin
- warping, caused by uneven drying during the seasoning process
- "shaking" or splitting, caused by the outside of the timber drying faster than the rest

All softwood takes glue, paint, and wood stain well, and has a pleasing finish when it is varnished or sealed with wax polish.

Reclaimed Floorboards

Reclaimed softwood floorboards are well-seasoned and have a pronounced grain pattern, as well as "character marks," which will have accumulated over many years of wear and tear. All these features can add to the interest of the finished piece and make it a particularly suitable choice for rustic country-style pieces, such as the Sewing Box and the Pull-along Duck (see pages 22 and 62).

Manufactured Fiberboards

New, good-quality softwood can be very costly, so in some cases we have suggested that you use a manufactured board instead of, or in combination with, wood.

Manufactured fiberboards are available in a wide variety of sizes and thicknesses.

MDF

MDF, or medium-density fiberboard, is an extremely versatile material. It is made from wood that has been reduced to its basic fiber particles and mixed with a synthetic resin adhesive and highly compressed. The density of the fiberboard is determined by the adhesive used and the degree of pressure applied.

MDF has a uniform structure with two smooth faces and can be sawn to give a clean, hard edge. It can be worked like wood and takes paint, lacquer, and varnish very well. MDF is heavier than softwood, but can still be joined in the same way, using glue and finishing nails or wood screws.

The only aesthetic drawback is its regularity, although moldings and paint effects can be applied to disguise its bland appearance.

We recommend that you wear a face mask when working with a power saw and MDF—especially for large projects—as the dust is considered to be a health risk when inhaled.

Plywood

Plywood is made by gluing layers of thin sheets of wood (plies), together, with the grain of each layer running in alternate directions to prevent warping. It is built up with an odd number of plies so that the outside grain runs in the same direction on both surfaces. The number varies according to the thickness of the plies and the finished board, but the minimum is three.

There are different grades of plywood depending on the quality of the outer veneers; the face plies (usually specified by a letter code) and the adhesives used in the laminating process. Check before you buy, because not all types of plywood are suitable for outdoor use. Choose a fine-quality ply to use for surfaces that will be visible, and a cheaper variety for drawer bases.

Never nail into the cut edge of plywood as it will cause the wood to split.

Balsa

Balsa is the softest and lightest of the commercial hardwoods. It is an open, straight-grained wood with a smooth appearance, which is very easy to sand and soft enough to be pierced with a bradawl.

Balsa can be bought in packs containing blocks of various shapes and sizes, and is perfect for small projects, such as the Clown Puppet (see page 71).

Molding or Beading

This decorative wood has a wide range of uses, from making picture-frame surrounds to adorning and finishing cut edges. A mitered molding around the base of a plain box, for example, makes it look far more solid and finished (see Sewing Box, page 22).

Doweling

These cylindrical rods of wood are used professionally for making joints. However, in these projects we have used them for hinging small items, such as the lid on the Candle Box (see page 36), and for decoration only, such as on the Pencil Box (see page 69). Doweling was also used to attach the wings and the wheels to the Pull-along Duck (see page 62).

When using doweling for hinging, select a diameter that is roughly one-third of the thickness of the timber into which it is to fit. Cut the dowel to size before fixing—aim for roughly one and a half times the thickness of the wood—and always drill the hole slightly longer than is necessary to ensure that it fits snugly.

You can buy wooden doweling in a range of sizes to suit your needs. If your local lumberyard doesn't stock the very narrow variety, try a model shop, or, alternatively, make use of ordinary matchsticks.

Tools & Equipment

If you are an experienced woodworker, you will already own a set of tools and know which one is best suited to a particular job.

The tools described here are the ones needed for basic woodworking, as the projects have been specially designed around a limited tool kit, but there are many more tools available to aid and delight the enthusiast.

Workbench

If space and money are no object, a good solid workbench is ideal for any carpentry project. Portable benches are useful for many jobs, and also double up as a large vise—the adjustable top can be opened up to hold timber for sawing, or laid flat to form a large work surface.

If you are new to woodcraft and don't have

access to a bench or vise, don't despair—all these projects can be completed on any stable work surface with the aid of clamps.

Clamping Equipment
Miter Clamps or Framing Clamps

By no means an essential set of equipment, but useful for clamping picture frames. The corners of the frame are covered with the four clamps and the cord is tightened to create tension and exert equal pressure on all four joints.

You can make an improvised version using strong cardboard, to protect the corners, and a length of twine wound twice around the frame. Insert a piece of dowel through the twine and twist it to tighten. This will hold the joined corners of the frame in place until the glue has bonded.

Clamps

We recommend using clamps to hold the wood in most of the projects, assuming that a beginner would be working on a tabletop, rather than a workbench equipped with a vise.

Clamps are available in a range of sizes defined by the width of their jaws. The jaws are tightened to hold surfaces together when sawing or gluing. When using clamps, always make sure you protect your wood from the metal jaws with pieces of scrap wood.

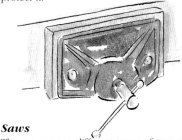

Vise

If you decide to invest in a workbench, make sure you choose one fitted with a carpenter's vise with wooden jaws. Failing this, you can buy removable vises that can be clamped onto a bench when required. If you use a vise with metal jaws, make sure you insert a piece of scrap wood on either side of your wood to protect it.

Saws

There are many different types of saw, some designed for basic carpentry, others for more specialist work. You will probably need several different types to complete these projects.

Coping Saw

This has a fine disposable blade tensioned within a frame and held in place by pins fitted through the blade which locate in notches in the saw's frame. It is used to cut curves in thin pieces of wood or for making internal cuts to remove waste wood. Choose a blade with fine teeth for intricate curves and one with coarser teeth for gentle curves.

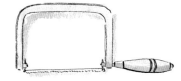

Handsaw

Many varieties of handsaws are available, which are used for general and specific purposes according to their length and the

number of teeth per inch (TPI). They include: the rip saw, a long saw (24–28 inches) with few TPI, normally 3–4, used for making long cuts in solid timber in the direction of the grain; the crosscut saw, a medium-length saw (22–26 inches) with 6–8 TPI, used for cutting solid timber or for cutting across the grain; and the panel saw, a short saw (18–22 inches), for fine-cutting of solid wood, both with and across the grain.

Saber saw

A very useful hand-held power tool, once you have learned to control it. A saber saw can be used for cutting intricate shapes and curves anywhere on a piece of wood. The blade moves up and down as it crosses the wood, always cutting on the upward stroke, which means that the smoothest cut will always be on the underside. Disposable blades come in many sizes and strengths, so make sure you

use the one most suited to your task—narrow blades are best for intricate shapes; wider ones for straight lines. A saber saw is not essential—if your wood is fairly thin, you should be able to make do with a coping saw instead.

Keyhole Saw

As its name suggests, this flexible hand-held saw is designed for small internal cuts, where a coping saw or saber saw would be inappropriate because of its size. It is worth keeping a number of spare blades because the teeth are easily damaged.

Tenon Saw or Backsaw

This all-round bench saw is ideal for small carpentry projects, where accuracy is essential,

and for cutting joints. The saw has a thin blade which is stiffened and weighted by a folded metal strip, usually brass, along the back edge. This prevents it bending, makes it easy to control, and allows for precision when cutting. It must always be used horizontally.

Tenon saws come in a great variety of sizes, the depth of the cut being limited by the height of the blade.

Drills and Bits

Power Drill

The drill is the most popular power tool, and it is assumed that every home has one these days. The most convenient type is the cordless,

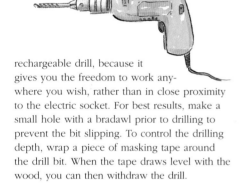

rechargeable drill, because it gives you the freedom to work anywhere you wish, rather than in close proximity to the electric socket. For best results, make a small hole with a bradawl prior to drilling to prevent the bit slipping. To control the drilling depth, wrap a piece of masking tape around the drill bit. When the tape draws level with the wood, you can then withdraw the drill.

Hand Drill

Power drills may take the hard work out of drilling, but they are not always easy to control, especially when working with very fine drill bits or when doing delicate work like drilling holes in wooden doweling. In this instance, you are better off with an old-fashioned hand drill, which offers greater control.

Drill Bits

You will need a selection of different bits in a range of sizes: twist bits for basic drilling; a countersink bit, so screw heads can be sunk into the wood; and a spade bit for making large holes. If you are drilling holes for wood screws, you will need at least two bits of different sizes to prevent the wood from splitting

when fixing the screws. The pilot hole should be narrower than the screw and slightly shorter than its length; the clearance hole should be fractionally wider and the same length as the screw shank (the smooth part of the screw).

Smoothing and Leveling Tools

File

Used for shaping the edges and simulating wear and tear when an antiqued finish is required. The most versatile type is the half-round file, which has a flat side and a rounded side. A file cuts on the forward stroke only, so push it across your work and then lift it for the return stroke. Wood must be clamped securely with a clamp or a vise.

Plane

A bench plane can be used to reduce the width or thickness of a piece of wood by shaving off thin layers, or to level or smooth a surface. It has a screw adjuster to regulate the depth of the cut and a lever to alter the angle of the blade. Light planing with a sharp and fine-set smoothing plane can produce an excellent finish. The smallest type of plane is the shoulder plane, and various other types are available for specialized cutting.

Abrasives and Sandpaper

Although sandpaper is the common name, various abrasives are used to make abrasive paper, which can be used for shaping, smoothing, and distressing wood or paintwork. Three grades are available—fine, medium, and coarse. Fine is best for smoothing and medium for shaping; coarse often scratches the wood's surface and is most suitable for removing paint. When sanding a flat surface, wrap the paper around a sanding block to ensure even pressure. Always sand with the grain, never against it.

Marking, Measuring and Cutting Tools

Bradawl (Awl)

This small tool is used to make starting holes for nails or screws. Its steel blade is either square- or diamond-shaped at the tip. For best results, press and twist to the right and left.

Chisel

Used, together with a mallet, for cutting grooves and rabbets, and for all kinds of trimming and shaping of wood. The size you need depends on the size of the groove or rabbet to be cut, so check the requirements before you buy. Blunt chisels cause more accidents than sharp ones, so always ensure that your chisel is sharp.

Craft Knife

A multipurpose tool; its main uses are to score a guideline to be followed by a saw, or to mark out a section to be removed with a chisel.

Miter Box

Available in metal, plastic or wood, miter boxes have slots for the saw blade with a left- and right-facing 45° angle at each end, and a right angle in the middle. The wood is placed inside the box and held or clamped against one of the sides. A tenon saw can then be slotted through to cut the wood at the required angle. This tool provides a foolproof aid to accurate mitering.

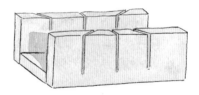

Level

A level is an essential piece of equipment to use when setting horizontal surfaces, such as fitting shelves, to ensure they are perfectly level. It is set so that the air bubble rests between two marks on the tube when it is horizontal.

Try Square

An L-shaped tool with a flat steel blade that is held at a right angle to a wooden or plastic handle. A try square is used for marking and checking right angles and parallel lines. Ensure that the handle is butted right up to the wood each time so that the angle is always 90°.

Hammers

A hand tool consisting of a heavy, usually steel, head held on the end of a handle. There are several different types on the market. The basic woodworking hammer is the cross-pein hammer and this is the one you should buy if you want to buy only one type. When driving a nail into wood, hold it between your fingers and start off using the tapered pein before driving the nail home with the flat head.

Claw Hammer

A general-purpose tool with a wooden or rubber handle. The claw is used to lever nails from wood. It is available in many sizes, identified by their head weight.

Cross-pein Hammer (peen)

A medium-weight cross-pein hammer can be used for all general carpentry work. It has a tapered pein at the back of the head, used for starting nails held between the fingers.

Mallet

Traditional carpentry mallets have wooden heads, essential for use with a chisel to prevent damage to the handle. Use the mallet to tap the end of the chisel's handle with even blows.

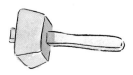

Pin Hammer

This small hammer is perfect for driving in finishing nails and small tacks or nails.

Nails

Nails come in many shapes and sizes (see above right). They should always be hammered through the thinner piece of wood into the thicker one and their length should be three times the thickness of the wood being fixed, so that two-thirds of their length is lodged in the thicker wood.

When hammering in a row of nails, stagger them rather than lining them up, which could cause splitting along the grain. If you are using nails to strengthen a glued joint, it is best to drive them in at alternate angles. This is called skew-nailing and it makes the joint much stronger.

Finishing Nails

Most of the nails used in the projects are small-headed finishing nails, which are almost invisible when hammered in place.

Cut Nails

These rustic-looking, angular nails are strong and well-suited to country-style woodwork. They come in a range of sizes.

Roundheaded Wire Nails

These nails should only be used for rough constructions, where they will not be visible.

Screwdrivers

It is important to choose the correct screwdriver to fit the size of the screw, by matching the width of the blade to that of the slot in the screw head. If the blade is too small or too large, the slot will chip or flatten altogether, making the screw difficult to remove.

Wood Screws

Screws, normally made of steel or brass, are classified by length and the thickness of the shank (or gauge). The length of the screw should be three times the width of the wood that is to be fixed. Head types are either flat-head or countersunk, which sit flush with the wood, or roundhead, which sit on the surface. Brass screws should be used with oak as steel is incompatible with oak and will cause the wood to stain. Choose a Phillips screw if you are using a power screwdriver, as this is less likely to slip than a slot-head screw.

When joining two pieces of wood with screws, always drill a hole first to take the screw. Start with a clearance hole larger than the screw's diameter and the length of its smooth shank. Then make a pilot hole slightly narrower than the screw's diameter and to just less than its depth. To ensure the correct drilling depth, wrap a piece of masking tape around the bit to indicate the screw's length. When this draws level with the wood surface, stop drilling. The clearance hole should always be drilled, but when you are screwing into softwood, you can make a pilot hole with a bradawl rather than a drill. There is also a hand-held tool called a gimlet that will start off a hole. This should be turned in one direction only, while pressure is applied. To remove the gimlet, twist it back the other way and it will have made a thread for the screw to lock into.

Hinges

Hinges are available in brass, steel, and nylon, and most are supplied in pairs. Butt hinges, made of two matching leaves, are the most common type of hinge and these are ideal for all the projects in the book.

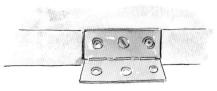

Adhesive

For simplification, when wood glue is specified in the projects, white woodworking glue is meant. Although it is known by many different trade names it is basically PVA (polyvinyl acetate), a thick water-based adhesive that is transparent when it dries. It is easily applied and sets at room temperature.

Always make sure that the surfaces of wood which are to be fixed fit each other properly and are free from dust. If necessary, smooth them with sandpaper first and then dust them with a soft cloth.

Apply sufficient glue to coat the wood but not so much that it drips and runs—too much glue will weaken the joint. Make sure that the whole surface of the joint is covered with a thin film of glue, then apply pressure by clamping for an hour. If you do not have clamps or a suitable vise, then the two pieces can be bound together with taut masking tape until the join has bonded. PVA is water-resistant but not weatherproof, so it should only be used for interior work if the finished work is not sealed.

Spray adhesive should be used for stenciling (see page 12), as it is not permanent, allowing you to peel the stencil away from your surface undamaged, to be used again. Spray adhesive is clean and easy to use and the residue left on your surface is minimal, but if you are spraying a large area, make up a cardboard spray-booth, as in the Letter Rack (see page 26). Always use spray adhesive sparingly, and apply it to the stencil rather than to the surface of the wood.

Painting Equipment

Acrylic Paints
Acrylic paints are suitable for use on most surfaces and are weatherproof once dry. They can be thinned with water, or mixed into any water-based medium, such as water-based varnish. Acrylics can be varnished, antiqued or waxed, making them very versatile. Another advantage is that brushes can be cleaned easily with water; but wash them out immediately as once the paint is dry it is impossible to remove.

Oil Paints
Oil paints are enjoyed for their depth of color and the transparency that can be achieved without a loss of color. Oil paints can be thinned with either distilled turpentine or an alkyd medium, such as polyurethane varnish. Alkyd oil color has a much shorter drying time than traditional oil paints, although it is still preferable to leave oils to dry overnight for the type of painting undertaken in these projects. To clean the brushes, soak in paint thinner, then wash in warm soapy water.

Latex Paints
Latex or emulsion paint can be used directly on sealed wood (a coat of shellac is the best sealant) to produce a matte, slightly chalky finish that looks particularly good on country-style woodcraft. Use latex paint for the background color, or even for applied patterns if you have the colors you need. To clean paintbrushes, simply wash under running water.

Varnish
The two types of varnish used in the projects are polyurethane (a tough, resin-based varnish) and acrylic (a water-based, milky colored varnish that dries clear in a short time). Both come in a range of finishes—matte, satin and gloss—and they can also be bought tinted or have color added to them. Remember that oil and water never mix, so use water-based varnish with acrylics or watercolors and polyurethane varnish with oil paints.

Shellac
An alcohol-based varnish which is available in a range of colors, from orange to clear. Shellac is useful for sealing bare wood or a painted surface. It has a relatively short drying time (1 hour) and is not waterproof.

Wood stain
Essentially a dye dissolved in alcohol that adds permanent color to the wood. Wood stain enhances the grain of the wood but will also be absorbed by any scratches or rough patches, so make sure the wood is well-sanded before application. Apply with a cotton cloth.

Paintbrushes
As a general rule, avoid cheap brushes. They don't keep their shape and can cause problems by shedding hairs into the paint. The artists' brushes used for these projects are made of a high-quality synthetic hair, which is durable with excellent shape retention. You will also require a set of good-quality household paintbrushes for applying color to larger areas, and a broad varnishing brush.

Stencil Cardboard
An oiled medium-weight cardboard that is water-repellent and can be wiped clean.

Maylar
The alternative stencil material—a sheet of transparent plastic—with the advantage of allowing you to see through to the surface below for accurate positioning. Although stencil cardboard is cheaper and a lot easier to cut than plastic sheeting, it is not so easy to bend when stenciling around the corner of a room.

Basic Techniques

These projects have been designed for people with a range of woodworking experience, although none require the skills of an expert. These are some of the basic techniques needed.

Templates
Enlarging Templates
Not all the templates are shown to the actual size and, in these cases, you will need to enlarge them to the correct dimensions on a photocopier. Simply zoom the control to the percentage given alongside the template.

Tracing Templates
The easiest way to transfer a template onto wood is using tracing paper. Lay the tracing paper over the template and, using a soft pencil (4B), draw around the outline onto the paper, making sure you include all positionals. Place the tracing face-down on scrap paper and shade over the traced outline on the reverse side. Position the tracing face-up on the wood and secure it with masking tape to prevent it from slipping. Draw over the outline to transfer the pencil markings onto the surface of the wood. If the design is intricate, it might help to score around the marked outline with a sharp craft knife to form a guide for the saw.

Making Joints
We have kept to three very basic types of joint. These are the butt joint, the lapped joint, and the mitered joint.

Butt Joint
This involves squaring off the ends to be joined, applying glue to one end grain, then lining it up with the side of the other piece. The joint is usually reinforced by nailing through from the back, but corner blocks can be inserted for extra strength, as in the Dolls' House (see page 84).

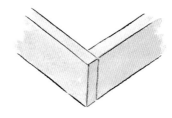

Lapped Joint

This joint involves trimming one side square and cutting a rabbet on the adjoining side. It is often used to fix drawer fronts. The rabbet is cut into the drawer front to the width a fraction less than the thickness of the drawer side that is to be slotted into it, to ensure a tight fit. Glue is applied to the rabbet and the sides are fitted, then nailed for extra strength.

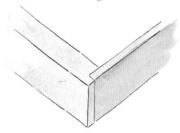

Mitered Joint

These joints are made with wood cut to a 45° angle along the end grain. The easiest way to cut the wood is using a tenon saw and a miter box. A mitered joint is very neat, making it ideal for frames and moldings (see pages 93–5). The cut edges are glued together and clamped with a miter clamp or frame clamp. For extra strength, the joint can be reinforced with finishing nails once the glue has dried.

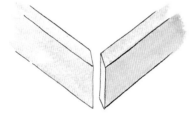

Sawing

You should always saw a piece of wood on the waste side of your cutting line. A handsaw should be used to saw your lengths of lumber to size before any fine work begins. Mark out a cutting line with a soft pencil against a try square, then score along the marked line with a craft knife—this will give the top edge of the wood a smooth finish. Use clamps or a vise to secure the wood when making the first few cuts—the idea is to make a channel for the saw blade to follow. Then remove the clamps and, holding the wood near to the blade with your spare hand, gently saw into the wood, keeping the blade lowered and supporting the wood from below for the last strokes. Always ensure that your saw is sharp.

Saber saw

This power tool is used for cutting straight lines or curves. To make a straight cut it is best to clamp a straight-edged piece of timber along the marked line to act as a guide for the saw blade. To cut a circle or curve, work in the

same way as you would with a coping saw (see below), by inserting the blade through a drilled hole and following a scored line. It is important that the base plate of the saw always remain in direct horizontal contact with the surface of the wood, otherwise vibration occurs and the blade can rip the wood. Practice is essential to get the feel of being in control of this tool, rather than letting it lead the way.

Tenon Saw

As with all saws, try to work with firm, even strokes, using the entire length of the blade. With a tenon saw, hold the blade horizontally to the wood and pull back on the first strokes to establish a start.

Coping Saw

This is used to cut curves and circles either on or near to the edge of a piece of wood. The depth you can cut is limited by the frame of the saw. If you are sawing a decorative or scalloped edge, mark out the shape first with a craft knife and secure the wood with clamps or a vise. Draw the blade of the saw away from the edge using short strokes.

If the saw is being used for an internal cut, drill a small hole through the work near the edge of the marked shape, then remove the blade and pass it through. Fit the blade back into the frame and cut out the shape. To make cutting easier, turn the blade within the frame.

Keyhole

This is useful for internal shapes, such as keyholes or circles. Because it is a simple, fine, tapered blade on a round handle, it can be used at any distance from

the edge, unlike the coping saw. To cut a circle, score the shape with a craft knife, then drill a hole near the edge and on the waste side of

your cutting line. Insert the blade through the hole and, holding it vertically, cut out the shape using short strokes and a moderate pressure.

Using a Plane

Make sure that the wood is held securely in place before you begin; when planing an edge, grip the wood in a vise, and when planing a flat surface, secure the wood to your work surface with clamps. A plane needs to be kept very sharp to work effectively. It cuts on the forward stroke, so work in one direction only, always following the grain of the wood.

Attaching Hinges

Before attaching a hinge to a piece of wood, ensure that it will lie flat. Position your hinge in the correct place and draw around it with a pencil. Measure the depth of the hinge, then chisel out the wood to this depth. If necessary, smooth the hollowed area with sandpaper so the hinge lies completely flat. To fix it, first drive a screw into the center hole on each side, making sure it is square, then fix the remaining screws on either side.

Making a Groove or Rabbet

If you don't own an electric router or a rabbet plane, the best way to cut a groove or rabbet is with a chisel and mallet. First mark out the area to be cut with a pencil, using a try square to draw two parallel lines. Score over the marked lines with a craft knife to form a channel for the saw. The depth of the groove or rabbet should be about one-third of the thickness of the wood that is to fit into it. Secure the wood to your work surface and saw along both lines to the correct depth. Choose a sharp chisel that will fit between the two lines and hollow out the waste wood, tapping the chisel's handle with a mallet to help you cut. Always work from the outer edge inwards, then rotate the wood and chisel towards the center from the other edge, so the groove or rabbet will be smooth and flat. If there is a large amount of waste wood to remove, drill several holes to the correct depth along the area before you start chiseling.

Index

Acknowledgments

The authors would like to express their appreciation and gratitude to folk artists and country craftspeople, past and present, whose work has been our inspiration. The "global supermarket" has brought a rich array of handmade and painted objects from all corners of the world into shops everywhere, but it would be a shame to replace making with shopping. We hope that this book will encourage you to experience the pleasure of the activity and the satisfaction of the end result.

We would also like to thank the following carpenters who assisted in the preparation of a number of the projects: Martin Abrahams, Ivan Carson and Tim Hickmott

Big thanks to Sacha, Josh, and Ray for all their help and friendship.

Finally, thanks to all at Ryland Peters & Small, whose high standards and good humor made this book a joy to create.